NICOPOLIS 1396

THE LAST CRUSADE

Ο ΜΕΡΚΟΥΡΙΟ

SERIES EDITOR: LEE JOHNSON

CAMPAIGN 64

NICOPOLIS 1396

THE LAST CRUSADE

TEXT BY
DAVID NICOLLE PhD

BATTLESCENE PLATES BY
CHRISTA HOOK

First published in Great Britain in 1999 by Osprey Publishing ,
Elms Court, Chapel Way, Botley, Oxford OX2 9LP
Email: osprey@osprey-publishing.co.uk

ISBN 1 85532 918 2

Editor: Marcus Cowper
Design: Ken Vail Graphic Design, Cambridge

Colour birds-eye-view illustrations by Peter Harper
Cartography by the Map Studio
Battlescene artwork by Christa Hook
Origination by Valhaven Ltd, Isleworth, UK
Printed through Worldprint Ltd, Hong Kong

99 00 01 02 03   10 9 8 7 6 5 4 3 2 1

For a Catalogue of all books published by Osprey Military,
Automotive and Aviation please write to:

The Marketing Manager, Osprey Publishing Ltd., PO Box 140,
Wellingborough, Northants NN8 4ZA United Kingdom
Email: info@OspreyDirect.co.uk

The Marketing Manager, Osprey Direct USA, PO Box 130,
Sterling Hts., MI 48211-0130, USA
Email: info@OspreyDirectUSA.com

OR VISIT THE OSPREY WEBSITE AT:
http://www.osprey-publishing.co.uk

Artist's Note

Dedication

For Joey; maybe the first book you'll want to read – but I doubt it.

Key to military series symbols

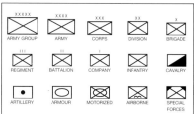

PAGE 2 **'St. Merkurios' on an early 14th-century Macedonian
wall painting. (*in situ* Church of St. Klement, Ohrid)**

TITLE PAGE **Some Italian artists, particularly those with
access to Venetian sketches, were accurate in their
portrayal of 'Turks'. These horsemen on an anonymous
painting of 'The Adoration of the Magi' could be Ottoman
akinci light cavalry. (Museo Civico, Padua)**

CONTENTS

ORIGINS OF THE CAMPAIGN

The background to the Nicopolis Crusade is to be found in the rapid spread of Ottoman Turkish conquests, particularly in the southern Balkans during the second half of the 14th century. More specifically, an Ottoman threat to Hungary following the failure of a Hungarian attempt to promote an uprising against Ottoman domination in Bulgaria, provoked action. At this time the Byzantine Empire consisted of Constantinople (with some adjoining coastal areas), southern Greece and some northern Aegean islands. Little was left of the Crusader States in Greece while Bulgaria had fragmented into smaller kingdoms which soon fell under Ottoman domination. The fragile Serbian Empire had similarly fragmented as the Ottomans thrust into the heart of the Balkans.

It proved almost impossible for the Orthodox Christian Balkan states to join forces with the Catholics to the north. Although the ruling elite often looked northward for help, most ordinary people seemingly

A Byzantine naval flag of c.1411. It shows the Emperor Manuel kneeling before the Archangel Michael. (Galleria Nazionale delle Marche, Urbino)

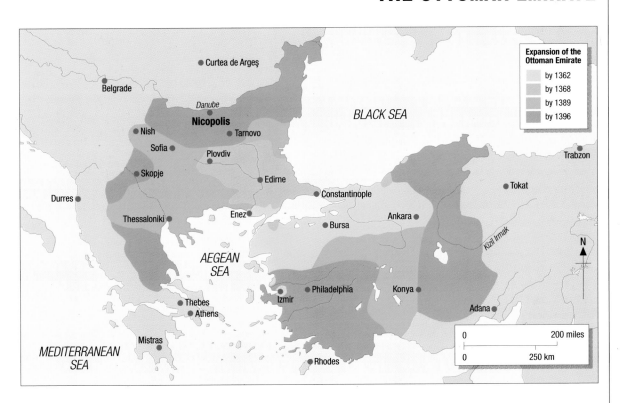

Expansion of the Ottoman Emirate

- by 1362
- by 1368
- by 1389
- by 1396

preferred Ottoman Islamic domination to that of the Catholic Hungarians. There was similar friction between the Orthodox Rumanians of Wallachia and Moldavia and their Catholic Hungarian overlords.

Within the fragmented relics of the Byzantine Empire this confusion reached epidemic proportions. More often than not the Emperors were now vassals of the Ottoman ruler and everywhere there was hostility between military and civilians, ruling elite and common people. Although the peasant and urban revolts of the mid-14th century had been crushed, they left large parts of Thrace and Macedonia almost uninhabited, except for a few fortified towns which were little more than fortified citadels surrounded by vegetable plots to feed their largely unpaid garrisons.

Meanwhile Ottoman expansion seemed carefully planned and was carried out with utter conviction. Some of the first Turks to seize territory in the Balkans were not actually Ottomans, but these early arrivals were rapidly absorbed by the more powerful Ottoman state. Its first capital was at Bursa in Anatolia but, perhaps after briefly using Didimotihon as their first European capital, the Ottomans made Edirne the base from which the greatest wave of Ottoman conquests was launched. Constantinople would not, of course, fall to the Ottomans until 1453. The Ottoman advance may have seemed inexorable but in the 1380s they did suffer setbacks. Most fighting was done by armies based upon three frontier *Uc* or marches: one thrusting north-east through Thrace being under the command of the ruler; one moving north-west through Bulgaria under Qara Tîmurtāsh; one forging west into Greece commanded by Gāzî Evrenos.

Meanwhile Prince Vlad of Wallachia thought of using Ottoman help in winning independence from Hungary, but his rival Mircea was more wary. Instead he seized the old Bulgarian Despotate of Dobruja to give his principality access to the Black Sea and made a treaty with Poland in 1389. In response the Ottoman commander Ali Paşa Cāndārli seized Nicopolis on the Danube and in 1391 the Ottomans launched their first raid north of the river. This forced Mircea back into an alliance with King Sigismund of Hungary and, perhaps in 1392, Mircea and Sigismund jointly retook Nicopolis. A new Balkan-Christian coalition seemed to be in the making but the following year Bāyazîd, the Ottoman ruler, re-imposed his authority in a lightning campaign. The Bulgarian Kingdom of Tarnovo was absorbed while Vidin and Serbia returned to their status as Ottoman vassals, though Bāyazîd also cultivated Serb friendship as a buffer against Hungary.

During this period the virtually empty plains of Thrace and eastern Macedonia were settled by the surplus population of Anatolia. These included several nomadic groups who became the *yürük* warrior-herdsmen of several mountainous regions. The role of Bektāshi dervishes who accompanied many Ottoman armies was also more important than is generally realised; not only acting as Islamic missionaries but also promoting the colonisation and re-cultivation of land devastated by war. The Bektāshis' relaxed attitude towards wine and the mixing of the sexes also eased relations with their Christian neighbours, so that by the end of the 14th century, Muslims, both Turkish newcomers and local converts, were a majority in Thrace.

Sigismund, Emperor of Germany and King of Hungary, in an early 15th-century portrait by Dürer. (Germanisches Nationalmuseum, inv. Gm. 168, Nürnberg)

The importance of Italian colonial outposts in the Black Sea during the Nicopolis campaign has not been fully recognised. The Black Sea itself was one of the world's major trade arteries with the Crimea at the centre of this network of communications. Italians dominated the sea and, although they frequently fought each other, this meant that Latin Crusader expeditions enjoyed naval superiority well into the 15th century. By the late 14th century Genoa was the major maritime power, with Genoese outposts forming a commonwealth of largely autonomous colonies. From here merchants and adventurers penetrated far up the great rivers of eastern Europe. In fact, an island fortress near Giurgiu, only a hundred kilometres from Nicopolis, may have been of Genoese origin and Genoese ships probably sailed up river as far as the Iron Gates on the border of Hungary.

The Kingdom of Hungary was unlike its western allies on the Nicopolis Crusade. Cultural differences between its regions were huge, ranging from the Catholic Magyars (Hungarians) in the centre and west, to Catholic Slovakian Slavs in the north, assorted Catholic and Orthodox

Slavs in the south, and the mixed Catholic and Orthodox region of Transylvania in the east. Transylvania actually retained its semi-autonomous status but settlement by Saxon immigrants and the activities of friars who tried to impose Catholic Christianity on the Orthodox population led to increasing tension. Some local *voivodes*, or princes, accepted Hungarian culture and Catholicism but others emigrated with their military retainers to Moldavia and Wallachia. The southern border was even more fluid with Hungarian rule in Croatia, Dalmatia and the Macso region of Serbia usually being effective while Hungarian authority in Bosnia was more superficial.

Moldavia and Wallachia sometimes accepted Hungarian suzerainty. Here in the mountains and foothills Rumanian-speaking leaders held sway but on the adjoining plains nomadic peoples of Turkish origin had only recently accepted Moldavian or Wallachian rule. The same was true of Slav communities living along some great rivers.

Both Moldavia and Wallachia had grown rich by controlling important trade routes and while Moldavia expanded north-eastwards into what had been Mongol Golden Horde territory, Wallachia wanted direct access to the Black Sea. By the late 14th century Wallachia also reached its cultural and political peak under the *voivode* Mircea the Elder. Nevertheless its status remained unclear; its political and military structures fragile.

The ruins of the Golden Gate in the land walls of Istanbul (Constantinople). (Author's photograph)

Even Hungary was weaker than it appeared. When Louis the Great of Hungary and Poland died in 1382 he left a formidable widow, Elisabeth, and two daughters: Maria aged eleven and Hedwig aged nine. Maria was crowned the day after Louis was buried but the Poles refused to recognise her as their Queen. After prolonged argument they accepted Hedwig instead; thus ending the brief union between Hungary and Poland. After Hedwig married Prince Jagiello this union was replaced by another between Poland and Lithuania. Unfortunately Maria was already engaged to Sigismund of Luxembourg, Margrave of Brandenburg and son of Emperor Charles IV of Germany. He never really accepted the loss of Poland, which he had hoped to rule along with Hungary. As Sigismund and Maria were in no hurry to marry, Hungary was ruled by the Queen Mother, Elisabeth. To further complicate the issue King Charles of Naples, ruler of southern Italy and adopted son of Louis the Great, maintained that he should be King of Hungary. In 1385 he invaded Dalmatia, Maria was forced to abdicate but Charles was assassinated by followers of Queen Mother Elisabeth. Charles' supporters then joined Tvartko, the *ban*, or governor, of Bosnia, in rebellion helped by the Venetians. Maria was captured and Elisabeth poisoned, whereupon Sigismund entered the fray, freed Maria and had

BELOW LEFT **'The Guards of Anushîrvan'** in a collection of poems illustrated in Baghdad in the same year as the Battle of Nicopolis. (Brit. Lib., Ms. Add. 18113, London)

BELOW RIGHT **Warrior saints on a wall painting in Albanian style, 1338–50. Though traditional, one saint wears a stylised 14th-century visored basinet.** (*in situ* Monastery Church, Decani, Kosovo Autonomous Region; author's photograph)

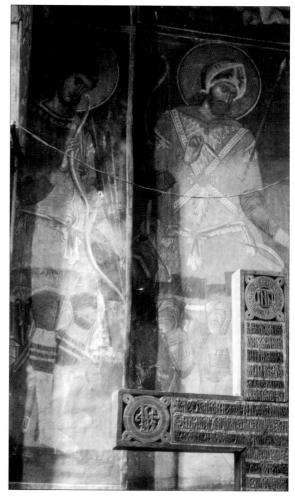

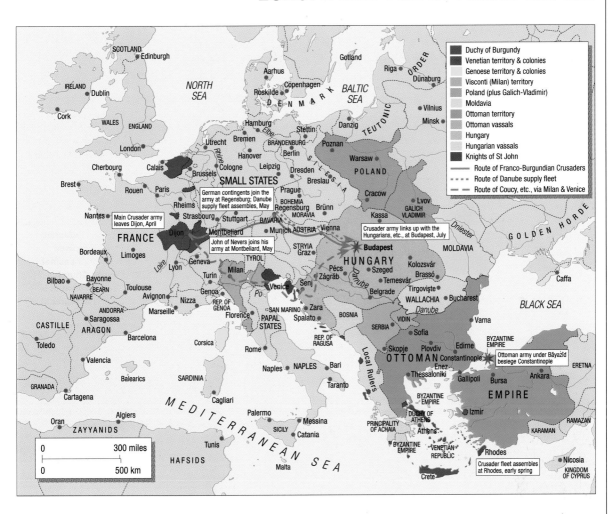

Map legend:
- Duchy of Burgundy
- Venetian territory & colonies
- Genoese territory & colonies
- Visconti (Milan) territory
- Poland (plus Galich-Vladimir)
- Moldavia
- Ottoman territory
- Ottoman vassals
- Hungary
- Hungarian vassals
- Knights of St John
- —— Route of Franco-Burgundian Crusaders
- ····· Route of Danube supply fleet
- – – – Route of Coucy, etc., via Milan & Venice

German contingents join the army at Regensburg; Danube supply fleet assembles, May

Main Crusader army leaves Dijon, April

John of Nevers joins his army at Montbeliard, May

Crusader army links up with the Hungarians, etc., at Budapest, July

Ottoman army under Bāyazîd besiege Constantinople

Crusader fleet assembles at Rhodes, early spring

himself crowned King in 1387. Eight years later Maria died. Many Hungarians now thought that the German Sigismund had lost his right to rule and rose up in rebellion. Though Sigismund crushed these rebels, his rule was more like that of the president of a league of senior barons than an autocratic monarch. Meanwhile he had to face the menace of Ottoman expansion and, during the second part of his reign, Sigismund was also Emperor of Germany.

As the Ottomans drew closer, the Hungarians tried to improve relations with their Orthodox subjects and gave Mircea of Wallachia the strategic Transylvanian Duchy of Fagaraş and County of Severin. Nevertheless, the events of 1391 and 1392 convinced Sigismund that Hungary needed help from western Europe. They also convinced Bāyazîd that the Bulgarian vassal Kingdom of Tarnovo was unreliable. While Sigismund called for a Crusade, Bāyazîd crushed Tarnovo and executed its king. The Danubian frontier castles at Silistria, Nicopolis and Vidin were strengthened and Muslims were encouraged to settle in the strategic Danube region. For their part the Hungarians and Wallachians regained the outpost of Nicopolis Minor on the north side of the river.

Bãyazîd still did not feel that the Ottoman position was secure, so in the winter of 1393–4 he summoned his Christian vassals to a conference at Serres in northern Greece. Here he selected Stefan Lazarevic of Serbia as his most trusted vassal while Emperor Manuel II became convinced that Byzantium was doomed unless he summoned help from the West. As soon as he returned to Constantinople, Manuel threw off Ottoman suzerainty and prepared to endure a new siege. This was not long in coming and it would last, on and off, for eight years. The Ottomans did not have the great cannon that would smash the walls of Constantinople half a century later, and Bãyazîd was also worried by Tîmur-i Lang's (Tamerlane) bloody campaigns to the east.

As the Ottomans besieged Constantinople, clashes increased along the Danube frontier. One probably included the battle of Rovine, though there is still debate about its actual date. It seems to have resulted from an Ottoman raid into Transylvania and Wallachia early in 1395. Here Bãyazîd attacked seven Hungarian fortified towns and castles before a bloody battle with Mircea's troops near the river Arges probably on 17 May. The Wallachians claimed a victory but the Ottomans held the field and briefly placed Mircea's rival Vlad on the Wallachian throne. They also installed garrisons at Nicopolis Minor and Giurgiu.

Effigy of the German knight Conrad von Seinheim, who died in 1369. (*in situ* Church of St. John, Schweinfurt; author's photograph)

Clearly Mircea had lost control of territory he held south of the Danube, and Sigismund now redoubled his efforts to get help from Western Europe. His ambassadors toured the major European powers, confirming treaties with France, Venice and various German princes, as well as Manuel of Byzantium and Mircea of Wallachia. They also got a favourable response from England, the Hospitallers and from Aragon, which ruled Sicily and part of Greece. On the other hand, Sigismund seems to have envisaged a defensive or pre-emptive campaign rather than a full-scale invasion of Ottoman territory. Western monarchs had more ambitious dreams and in May King Charles of France sent a letter to Richard II of England saying: 'Then, fair brother, it will be fair moment ... that you and I, for the propitiation of the sins of our ancestors, should undertake a Crusade to succour our fellow Christians and to liberate the Holy Land …'.

A more immediate result of these agreements was the raising of special taxes – the Duke of Burgundy pulling in the huge sum of 700,000 gold francs – while the Hungarians returned home bearing encouraging news. Certainly the Hungarians had been lucky in arriving during a four-year truce in the Hundred Years War between France and England. Help was promised from all sides, yet it was the Burgundians who took the lead and bore the main burden. Duke Philip wanted to avoid involvement in any renewed Anglo-French hostilities and he also saw the Crusade as a way of demonstrating Burgundy's new-found power. In 1394 he had already sent an armed delegation, under Guillaume de la Trémoille and Regnier Pot, to

A late 14th-century bronze pendant in the form of a seated nobleman, found in the ruins of Curtea de Arges, Wallachia. (Muzeul Național Cotroceni, Bucharest)

assess the situation in Hungary. They returned to take part in military discussions in the Hôtel d'Artois in Dijon.

There Duke Philip's son, John of Nevers, promised to dedicate his first feat of arms to the service of God. He also volunteered to lead the Crusade and, despite his inexperience and a broken shoulder (the result of a recent riding accident), this was agreed in August 1395. A celebratory mass was held in the Cathedral of St. Denis in Paris but even now Count John of Nevers was not knighted because: 'He was to receive the accolade like a knight of Jesus Christ at the first battle against the infidels.' In reality John of Nevers' role was nominal while real command was placed in the hands of the Count d'Eu. Other senior advisors would include the Admirale de Vienne, Marshal Boucicault, the two Sires de Bar, the Comte de la Marche, plus the Sires de Saimpy, de Roye and de la Trémoille.

Enthusiasm for the Crusade was widespread and genuine, so much so that only the aristocratic elite were actually allowed to join the army. The Burgundian chamberlains put enormous effort into arraying the Crusaders in brocade clothing, gilded and silvered harness, supplying the Count of Nevers' units with green satin tents and tunics. Armour and tableware were also the most magnificent available. The Hospitallers were also keen to join the Crusade since their garrisons at Rhodes, Izmir and other parts of the Aegean felt threatened by the Ottomans. Philibert de Naillac, Hospitaller Grand Prior in Aquitaine, agreed to support the Crusade and left for Rhodes with reinforcements. Boniface X, the Pope in Rome, was enthusiastic, as was his rival, Benedict XIII, the Pope in Avignon. The Venetian Senate agreed to join the Crusading League, though only at sea, while Venetian ambassadors secretly tried to mediate between the Ottomans and Byzantines, since hostilities endangered trade. In February 1396 the Byzantines apparently agreed to supply ten war galleys, built in Venice for use in the Danube area, though in the event they do not seem to have taken part.

This was a new kind of Crusade, with secular rulers taking the lead as Popes tagged along behind. Crusading enthusiasm was virtually dead amongst ordinary people but the almost contradictory ideals of Crusading and Chivalry had finally merged into one among the aristocracy. As the famous Burgundian poet Eustache Deschamps wrote around 1395:

'Princes mondain, je vous requier et proy
Que vous m'aidiez les Sarrasins conquerre:
Je suis la loy, soiex avecques moy
Pour conquerir de cuer de Sainte Terre.'

[Princes today, I ask you and pray that you will help me to conquer the Saracens: I am the law, come with me to conquer the heart of the Holy Land.]

THE OPPOSING COMMANDERS

CRUSADER LEADERS

Sigismund, Margrave of Brandenburg and second son of the German Emperor Charles IV, was born in 1368. Betrothed to Mary, daughter of King Louis of Hungary, Sigismund became ruler of Hungary in 1387. In 1410 he was also elected Emperor of Germany and, ten years later, King of Bohemia. He died in 1437. Sigismund was a man of huge ambition and energy. He promoted Crusades against the Ottoman Turks, tried to heal Schisms within the Catholic Papacy and between Catholic and Orthodox Churches, tried to end the Hundred Years War between England and France, and fought the 'heretical' Hussites of Bohemia. Though few of his projects succeeded, Sigismund's reign saw a considerable expansion of towns and trade in Central Europe.

Mircea 'The Old' of Wallachia also earned the title of 'The Great'. He came to power as *voivode* in 1386 and set about extending Wallachian territory towards the Black Sea. He joined the Balkan-Christian alliance which was defeated by the Ottomans at the battle of Kosovo in 1389. But, like most medieval Wallachian rulers, Mircea switched allegiance back and forth between Hungary and the rising Ottoman Empire in an effort to preserve Wallachian autonomy. He also had to fight rival leaders who, like himself, were used as political pawns by Wallachia's powerful neighbours. He had little choice but to take part in the disastrous Crusade of Nicopolis. After the massive Ottoman defeat by Tîmur-i Lang in 1402, Mircea supported various rival Ottoman princes as they struggled for control of the shattered Ottoman state. Once the Ottomans regained their stability, however, Wallachia became an Ottoman vassal state – though probably after Mircea died in 1418. Outside Wallachia, Mircea's reputation varied considerably; among the Crusaders at Nicopolis, only Enguerrand de Coucy seems to have befriended him, while the Ottomans

'Knights enact a mock assault upon a Saracen castle during the feast in the Great Hall of the Palais de la Cité, Paris', French manuscript c.1378–80. (*Grand Chroniques de France***, Bib. Nat., Ms. Fr. 2813, f.473v, Paris)**

The signature of Mircea, the *voivode* of Wallachia, at the bottom of a manuscript dated 1415 AD. (Arhivele Naționale, Bucharest)

An almost unique three-dimensional representation of a mounted warrior from 14th-century Serbia. Unlike wall paintings in archaic Romano-Byzantine armour, this man is equipped much like an Italian light cavalryman. (*in situ* Narthex of Radoslav, Monastery Church, Studenica; author's photograph)

regarded him as 'the most courageous and shrewd among the Christian princes'.

John, son of Duke Philip of Burgundy, was born in 1371 and spent most of his early life in Flanders. His Flemish motto was 'Ic houd' (I never give up). John started to play a public role as early as 1384 and was almost immediately made Count of Nevers. Six weeks before his 14th birthday he married Margaret of Bavaria and for the next few years he was attached to his father's household, gaining military and political experience. John became Duke of Burgundy in 1404, Count of Flanders and Artois in 1405. He was described as, 'a small dark man with blue eyes, a full face, an unfaltering glance, and uncompromising jaw … and a massive squashed head'. Whether he really earned his nickname of 'The Fearless' at the battle of Nicopolis is disputed but he was the only 14th–15th-century Burgundian ruler to handle an army successfully. He was considered coarse, lacking charm and having no interest in the elaborate clothes which preoccupied most French noblemen. Brave, wily and ambitious, he also liked to inspire fear. Unfortunately John's reign as Duke was dominated by his quarrel with Louis of Orléans, resulting in a decade of civil war between the Burgundian and Armagnac factions which allowed the English to ravage France. He was assassinated in 1419.

The De Naillac family was one of the most important in the Berry area of central France. Philibert became the most famous but as a younger son he had to seek his fortune elsewhere, choosing to enter the Military Order of Hospitallers. By 1383 he was Grand Prior of the Order in the Aquitaine. Philibert de Naillac was helping distribute the family estates among his brothers when the call came for a Crusade. He was sent to the main Hospitaller headquarters on the island of Rhodes, where, in March, the Grand Master Ferdinand de

15

Hérédia suddenly died. Philibert de Naillac was now elected Grand Master, and almost immediately led a squadron of Hospitaller war galleys with the rest of the Crusader fleet to the mouth of the Danube. After his return to Rhodes, Philibert de Naillac commanded a small fleet which continued to give the Ottomans trouble in the Aegean as well as ravaging the coasts of Mamluk-ruled Lebanon. He died in 1421.

OTTOMAN LEADERS

Bāyazîd I was born in 1354, son of the Ottoman ruler Murad I and Gül-chichek 'Rose Flower' Khatun, who some sources say was Greek. He was appointed governor of a recently conquered Anatolian province around 1381 and within a few years was responsible for Ottoman affairs throughout the East. Bāyazîd earned a reputation as a brave but impetuous soldier, probably earning his nickname of *Yildirim,* 'The Thunderbolt', after defeating the Qaramānids in 1386. He was recognised as ruler following the assassination of Murad during the battle of Kosovo, after which Bāyazîd married Maria (also known as Despina or Olvera), a daughter of King Lazar of Serbia (who was also killed at Kosovo). Maria's brother Stefan Lazarevic, the new Serbian ruler, remained a loyal vassal and friend until Bāyazîd's death. The only war that Bāyazîd lost was his last, when he was captured by Tîmur-i Lang (Tamerlane) at Ankara in 1402. He died in captivity the following year. Apart from being a noted

Some Italian artists, particularly those with access to Venetian sketches, were accurate in their portrayal of 'Turks'. These horsemen on an anonymous painting of 'The Adoration of the Magi' could be Ottoman *akinci* light cavalry. (Museo Civico, Padua)

'St. George', gilded and painted wooden statue by Jacques de Baerze, Burgundian 1390–99. (Musée des Beaux Arts, Dijon)

soldier, Bãyazîd was one of the first Ottoman rulers to be a patron of literature. He also supported mystical Islamic groups, his daughter Nilüfer 'Water-lily' reputedly married the leader of the Suhrawardi dervishes.

Secondary leaders played only a minor role in the highly centralised Ottoman military system. Nevertheless they included some talented commanders. The most senior was the grand vizier or 'prime minister' Qara Tîmurta<u>sh</u>, son of the famous warrior Qara Alî Beg. Tîmurta<u>sh</u> himself was first mentioned during the reign of Murad, leading an Ottoman army along the Tunca river. Thereafter he conquered much of eastern Bulgaria and became the *Beglerbeg* or military commander of Ottoman territory in Europe. In this role he established two elite cavalry regiments called the *Ulufeciyan* (regular or salaried troops) and recruited local *voinaks* or Christian soldiers. His courage earned him the right to have a standard with three horse-tails, the first *Beglerbeg* to do so. A few years later he also earned Bãyazîd's unspoken gratitude by executing a dangerous rival, who happened to be Bãyazîd's brother-in-law. Tîmurta<u>sh</u> was murdered in 1405, during the anarchic civil wars which racked the Ottoman state after Bãyazîd's death and was buried in a mosque he had founded in Bursa.

The career of Gãzî Evrenos Beg was even more dramatic. According to some sources, Evrenos, son of 'Îsã (Jesus) Beg Prangi, came from a family of Byzantine origin that had transferred its allegiance to the Turkish Qarasï rulers and converted to Islam early in the 14th century. Gãzî Evrenos was among troops sent by Orkhan to help the Byzantine Emperor Cantacuzenos during a civil war against the rival Emperor John V. After the Ottomans won a foothold on the European side of the Dardanelles in 1354, Evrenos became one of their most successful commanders in the Balkans. He continued to be successful under no less than five Ottoman rulers, becoming *Uc-Beg* or governor of the 'Left March', extending Ottoman control to Thessaloniki, Macedonia, Albania and finally down into the heartlands of Greece itself. Unlike most other leading Ottoman commanders of that time, Gãzî Evrenos was a relatively orthodox Muslim, making the Haj pilgrimage to Mecca and promoting the establishment of mosques, *madrasah* religious schools, *imaret* hostels for the poor, dervish convents, *hamam* public baths and *caravanserai* hostels for merchants. Under his governorship Komotini, in what is now north-eastern Greece, became one of the first centres of Turkish-Islamic culture in Europe. He died on 17 November 1417; a dedicatory inscription on his tomb at Yenitsa states: 'Transported from this Transient World to the Realm of Permanence, the receiver of God's mercy and forgiveness, the blessed, the martyr, the king of the Gāẑîs [religiously motivated warriors] and the fighters of Jîhad, slayer of the infidels and the polytheists, ... Haji Evrenos son of Îsa, may God illuminate his grave and may his dust be fragrant, to the mercy of Almighty God and His approval'.

Stefan Lazarevic was the most loyal of Bāyazîd's Balkan vassals. Born around 1373, he inherited his father's role as *Krales* or Prince of Serbia following Lazar's death at Kosovo in 1389. He was still very young and his mother, the regent Milica, probably arranged the marriage between Stefan's sister and Bāyazîd. Thereafter Stefan and Bāyazîd became comrades-in-arms until Bāyazîd was captured at Ankara. Stefan escaped Tîmur-i Lang's clutches and, on his way home, he visited Constantinople, where the Emperor Manuel gave him the official title of *Despot* of Serbia. Civil war amongst rival Ottoman princes enabled Stefan to extend Serbian territory. He also became a vassal of Hungary and received Belgrade as a reward from Sigismund around 1403. In his later years Stefan Lazarevic re-established good relations with the Ottomans but died without issue in 1427 and was buried in the monastery he himself founded at Resava.

Late 14th-century Western European armour.
TOP LEFT **Northern Italian breastplate showing rivets that would have secured a thick velvet covering (Monastery of S. Lazzaro, Venice, photograph M. Morin).**
BOTTOM LEFT **Italian barbuta (Askeri Muze, inv. 7062, Istanbul, author's photograph).**
RIGHT **Italian basinet lacking its visor (Royal Armouries, Leeds).**

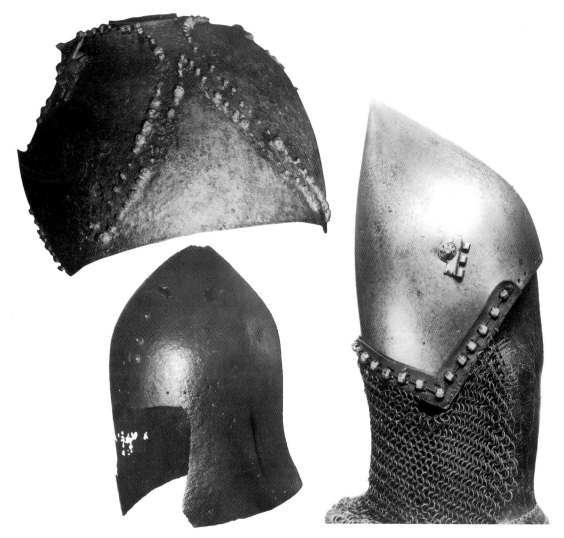

OPPOSING FORCES

CRUSADER ARMIES

France was the richest country in Europe during the 14th century. The feudalism of the 12th–13th centuries had given way to so-called 'bastard feudalism' under which knights and squires served in return for payment rather than merely because of feudal obligation. There was also an artificial revival of chivalric ideas as the old aristocracy struggled to maintain a social order threatened by an increasingly wealthy middle class. Meanwhile warfare remained one of the routes by which the brave, capable and lucky could win advancement.

Of all the fragmented regions of France, Burgundy was emerging as one of the most powerful. Its Duke rivalled the King in military might, and his acquisition of Flanders gave control of one the economic powerhouses of medieval Europe. Within Burgundy the Duke's military power was built around his 'household', which formed a standing army. Its nucleus consisting of heavily armoured men-at-arms capable of fighting on horseback or on foot. A smaller contingent consisted of mounted archers and crossbowmen (who were really mounted infantry), plus a few light cavalry.

Although the Crusading army of 1396 included few archers and crossbowmen, the proportion in the retinue of the Count of Nevers (13.6 per cent) was actually bigger than in previous Burgundian armies. Nevertheless, the prevailing tactical emphasis was on heavily armoured men-at-arms. Furthermore the ideological context of the Crusade worked against the use of archers and crossbowmen, resulting in overwhelmingly offensive tactics ill-suited to cope with Ottoman warfare.

This reliance on armoured cavalry also reflected Burgundian society, where the old aristocracy remained more deeply entrenched than in most other parts of Europe. In fact, the Burgundian knightly elite believed that they enjoyed an even

The Mace Tower on one corner of Buda Castle overlooking Budapest. (Author's photograph)

19

higher status than the knights of other lands. Men who had only recently been ennobled, even as a result of great heroism, prowess and loyalty, were still supposed to remain modestly in the background when in the presence of those with longer pedigrees. One result of this code was that loyalty and duty overrode all other considerations; honour being far more important than life itself. Honour dictated that battle should never be refused, but common sense suggested that it could. The result was tortured consciences and sleepless nights for many commanders.

An increase in the importance of infantry seen earlier in the 14th century had to some extent been reversed by the 1390s, particularly in France, Burgundy and Germany. It is also important to note that most of the so-called Genoese crossbowmen seen in French armies were not of Genoese origin, though they had been recruited via Genoa. In Burgundian armies transport was supplied by large numbers of wagons which, of course, were looked after by an even greater number of wagoners. Nevertheless, the Danube provided the Crusaders with their main means of transport, large numbers of river craft being assembled at Regensburg in Bavaria. Other ships were added to the fleet at Budapest and perhaps Vienna while the heavy equipment was to be brought by a Crusader fleet sailing up the Danube from the Black Sea.

The morale of the Franco-Burgundian contingent was based upon the knights' overriding belief in their own military superiority; their attitude towards warfare being summed up by the Burgundian poet Eustache Deschamps back in 1386: 'Vaillant cuer peut en tout temps

John the Fearless, Duke of Burgundy, on an anonymous early 15th-century Franco-Flemish panel painting. (Musée du Louvre, Paris)

A farm on the Great Plain of Hungary, east of Budapest. Such countryside would have seemed strange to Crusaders from France or Germany. (Author's photograph)

faire guerre' (a brave heart is always ready to fight). Now their enthusiasm was even greater since they were embarking upon the most prestigious of all chivalrous activities – a Crusade. Unfortunately many of them regarded 'schismatic' Greek Orthodox Christians and Muslims alike as foes. Even the famous Italian poet and humanist Petrarch had written that: 'The Ottomans are merely enemies but the schismatic Greeks are worse than enemies. The Ottomans hate us less, for they fear us less. The Greeks … however, both fear and hate us with all their soul'.

Painted wooden statue of St. George made in Bavaria around 1390. (Bayerisches Nationalmuseum, Munich)

The German contribution to the Crusade has sometimes been overlooked. Of course Burgundians took the leading role and France was still considered the fountainhead of chivalry. As a result the organisation of late 14th-century German aristocratic armies mirrored that of the French. The cavalry were usually organised into *gleven* that were virtually identical to the French *lances*. One example described in 1373 consisted of a fully armoured man-at-arms supported by a mounted crossbowman or archer and a mounted page. There were variations but in each case heavily armoured horsemen dominated.

Hungarian forces changed considerably during the 14th century. The new ruling dynasty of Angevin kings introduced Western European military systems and used the existing baronial armies, or *banderia*, as the basis of a new army. At the same time, however, relics of earlier military systems survived, including the *insurrectio* (or levy) of the entire knightly class, as well as special non-noble military groups (see below), and in an extreme emergency, a summoning of the entire male population. The result could be a remarkably varied army which differed from those seen in Western Europe. Its elite remained armoured cavalry like those of Germany or France, but Hungary could also field large numbers of light cavalry including numerous horse archers.

Even among the Hungarian feudal nobility, Western European concepts were often only skin deep. Links with the steppes to the east remained strong and the Hungarians still felt considerable affinity with Turks and other steppe peoples. Western feudal and chivalric influence was even more limited in Transylvania and the southern Slav provinces, where fighting forces mostly consisted of militias under their own local *knez* leaders. It was, in fact, the light cavalry that made Hungarian forces so distinctive. The bulk were drawn from the Székelys, a community whose origins remain a matter of nationalistic argument in Central Europe. They were divided into six clans and 24 lineages, each lineage providing a hundred elite light cavalrymen plus a militia. The Turkish Pechenegs settled in Hungary in relatively small numbers and were soon absorbed. The Kipchaqs, or Cumans as they were generally known, arrived in larger numbers, having been driven westward by the Mongols, and they had a profound military impact. Finally there were the Iasians, who were Iranian-speaking Ossetian, or Alan, rather than Turkish nomads, again driven from the steppes by the Mongols. Such people served as horse archers, though the feudalisation of their elite had led to a decline in their military importance by the late 14th century. Nevertheless, the need for light cavalry was clearly recognised, and in 1395 King Sigismund ordered that each Hungarian lance-armed heavy cavalryman should be accompanied by two mounted archers. Half a century after Nicopolis, Bertrand de la Brocqière noted that the Hungarians: 'use short strong lances … They joust one-to-one and always in pairs ... In the border territory between Austria and Bohemia there are light crossbowmen. In Hungary there are archers with bows like those of the Turks, but they are not as good or as strong. Nor are the people as good shots. The Hungarians shoot with three fingers and the Turks with the thumb and the ring finger'.

Though cavalry dominated Hungarian warfare, infantry still had a part to play and a large scale enlistment of mercenaries began during the Hungarian Kings' Italian wars in the later 14th century. These included crossbowmen, as Bertrand de la Brocqière reported on the battle of Nicopolis: 'He [King Sigismund] had 25,000–30,000 Hungarians with him but only 200 Lombard and Genoese crossbowmen'.

Sigismund is said to have envisaged a defensive campaign in 1396 and although this is unlikely to have been passive it would have relied on existing fortifications. Perhaps one reason why Sigismund so readily accepted the Crusaders' demand for an offensive was the poor state of Hungarian fortifications. By the late 14th century most such castles reflected baronial power, not national defence, and although an effort was made to strengthen the south-eastern frontier, most such work was done after the battle of Nicopolis.

Most accounts of the Nicopolis campaign described the Wallachians as unreliable allies who deserted at a crucial moment. In reality they were a significant force, though one whose loyalties were strained. The dominant people within the vulnerable *voivodate* of Wallachia were Rumanian-speaking Vlachs. Their society was tribal rather than feudal, largely consisting of transhumant pastoralists in the mountains and foothills. Meanwhile other peoples, including Turco-Mongol nomads, roamed the plains north of the Danube.

Wallachian military organisation may have been primitive but its troops were considered to be among the best warriors in the Balkans. Some fought as horse-archers; others were famed for their skill in woodland warfare. A large proportion consisted of mounted infantry called *voinici* or *Iunaci* while their cavalry elite were called *viteji* or 'knights'. A third source of troops was the *Străjeri* frontier guards, whose name stemmed from the Byzantine Greek term *stradiotai* (quasi-feudal elite). Together with a few foreign

The best preserved painting in the *Iskander Nameh*, made at Amasya in northern Anatolia in 1416. (Bib. Nat., Ms. Turc. 309, f.130v, Paris)

The Derdap Gorge leading to the Iron Gates was a major obstacle to navigation along the Danube. It formed a border between Catholic Central Europe and the Orthodox Balkans. Today the Gorge is flooded by a man-made lake. (Author's photograph)

mercenaries, this Wallachian military elite formed the *Curteni*, or households, of the *voivode* and his *boyar* senior aristocrats.

Mircea is credited with developing a permanent army based upon earlier part-time *Dorobanți* militia formations; a term stemming from the Turkish *derbendci,* meaning 'guardians of the passes'. The Wallachian *Oastea cel mare* or 'Big Army'" was also first mentioned in documents from Mircea's reign when it consisted of a general levy of free men from districts known as *Județe.* This may have existed as early as 1374, though the term *Oastea cel mare* did not appear until the start of the 15th century.

One major factor in the Nicopolis campaign is often overlooked. This was the Crusaders' overwhelming naval superiority, largely based upon the fleets of Venice and Genoa. Furthermore this domination extended far up the rivers which flowed into the Black Sea; significantly the Danube. The most important Genoese colony in the Black Sea was Kaffa, in the Crimea. Here the *Caput Gazarie* was responsible for the defence of all Genoa's Black Sea outposts. He commanded a well-equipped militia including numerous crossbowmen and even had his own small fleet. Italian galleys could raid enemy coasts almost at will and were quite capable of capturing small coastal fortifications. Compared to such a naval power the Crusading Order of Hospitallers was a minor player. Nevertheless, its influence was considerable. Its men were also the most fanatical Holy Warriors, cultivating a mystique of martyrdom and habitually killing Turkish Muslim prisoners while enslaving 'schismatic' Greeks.

OTTOMAN ARMIES

Ottoman society and its army were based upon the Persian-Islamic model, not on the nomadic Turkish heritage. The Ottoman military system also differed from that of most other Islamic societies because existing Balkan-Christian elites were accepted along with existing Turkish military elites in Anatolia. On the other hand, continuity from the Byzantine and Balkan-Christian past was more noticeable in frontier regions than in the central provinces, while in military terms it was more apparent in middle and lower ranks than at the command level.

At the centre was the ruler who was as yet only an *Amîr* rather than a *Sultan*. Outside his immediate *Harim* or domestic household was the *Birum* or 'outer service', which included guard units such as the famous *Yeni Ceri* Janissaries. All members of the *Birum* were known as *kul* or 'slaves' though in reality many were free. What astonished Western observers most, however, was the discipline of the entire military structure. As Bertrand de la Brocquière noted a generation later: 'There is no one so great as to dare to overreach his authority, on pain of death. I think this is one of the reasons why they have been so successful and conquered so much by war ...'

The elite professional units of the Ottoman army dated from the early days of the Ottoman state and again reflected Persian-Islamic rather than Turkish traditions. Cavalry dominated Ottoman armies, in prestige if not in numbers, and several new regiments were created during the 14th century. Those maintained by *timar* 'fiefs' were known as *timarli* while those paid directly by the state were called *maasli*. Meanwhile the increasing cost of warfare led to a bureaucratisation of the state in the later 14th century; making the Ottoman realm similar to established Islamic states in the Middle East. The number of troops each *timar* holder was expected to bring to muster varied but was written into

Lipova Castle was one of a series of small fortresses that protected the south-eastern frontier of medieval Hungary. (Author's photograph)

Jean de Meinge, Maréchal de Boucicault, with his wife Antoinette de Turenne, venerating the Madonna and Child. (*Heures du Maréchal de Boucicault,* Musée Jacquemart-André, Paris)

Geoffrey de Bouillon, the great hero of the First Crusade, on a late 14th- to early 15th-century Italian wall painting. (*in situ* Castello, Mantua)

the original donation. Nevertheless, this system had many features in common with Byzantine *pronoia* fiefs, so that it was easy for the Ottoman conquerors to convert existing *pronoias* and their Balkan counterparts into new *timars*.

Beyond the elite palace or guard regiments, the Ottoman army was divided into two parts based upon the Anatolian or eastern part of the state and the Rumelian or Balkan western part. Each was commanded by a *Beglerbeg*, '*Beg* of *Begs*', and beneath them were *Sancak Begs* in charge of military provinces. All these senior officers received their banners directly from the ruler and such banners symbolised the ruler's authority, not the status of the officer himself. As such they were entirely different to Western heraldic banners. There were, however, interesting parallels between Ottoman and Western forces, most notably at the lower levels. The Rumelian *Gönder*, for example, meant a small unit of three to five men summoned for service together. It probably came from the Greek *kontarion*, meaning a cavalry lance, and served the same purpose as the Western 'lance' cavalry unit.

The main source of 14th-century Ottoman military thinking was the Mamluk Sultanate of Egypt and Syria where the traditions of Islamic military theory, from broad strategy to individual weapons training, flourished. Most military texts were written in Arabic, which only the most educated Ottomans could understand. On the other hand Turkish was already the common language of the military elites in the eastern and central parts of the Islamic World as well as the

25

Eurasian steppes to the north. Some Mamluk military texts, including works on *furusiyya* (or military skills, in the broadest sense) were translated into Kipchaq Turkish, and it seems very likely that they eventually reached the Ottoman state.

The battle of Nicopolis can be interpreted as an example of classic Islamic tactics, in which a strong position was occupied, defended with field fortifications, and used as a basis from which to launch a counterblow. Other aspects of Ottoman military capability, which amazed and appalled Western observers, were their advance intelligence about an enemies' strength, movements and intentions, their command and control on the battlefield, as well as the discipline and sobriety of their soldiers.

To focus solely on Ottoman elite formations would be misleading, as the Ottoman army included large numbers of much less formidable warriors. Of the Turkish tribal forces, which had formed the backbone of earlier Ottoman armies, those that remained on call largely consisted of horse-archers grouped into *Ocaks,* or groups of men, one of whom went to war while his comrades remained at home to pay his expenses.

Most of those Turkish tribal forces that crossed into Europe in the second half of the 14th century soon evolved into *akincis,* or frontier warriors, where they were joined by part of the existing Christian military classes. Balkan pastoral peoples also proved a fertile recruiting ground for *akincis* and as a result these troops tended to speak local languages and to know the country well. They, like other Ottoman Balkan forces, were organised into units of the 'left' and the 'right' like regular Ottoman troops.

By the late 14th century *Müsellem* cavalry, raised by the first Ottoman rulers to supplement unpredictable Turkish tribal forces, had evolved into a mounted pioneer corps that rode ahead of an army to ensure that roads and bridges were in adequate condition. The bulk of Ottoman cavalry were now fief-holding *timarli,* often confusingly called *sipahis* like the elite palace cavalry regiments. They normally only served between March and October, returning home in winter to revive their horses and look after their estates. The 'fighting money' incomes from such *timars* could also be topped up with *teraqqî* (bonuses) to encourage good performance and promotion. Those with a higher valued *timar* brought up to five armed followers known as *jebeli* but all mustered and fought beneath the banner of their *Sancak Beg.* Furthermore a large proportion of Balkan *timarli* cavalry were still Christian, being members of existing warrior aristocracies which had accepted Ottoman rule.

The best Ottoman cavalry were a palace corps of six *Bölükat* or Regiments under the rulers immediate command. Most were again

This damaged early 15th-century manuscript from Amasya in northern Turkey shows three horsemen with pointed helmets, two carrying spears while their leader has a mace and a bowcase. (*Iskander Nameh,* Bib. Nat., Ms. Turc. 309, f.295v, Paris)

called *sipahîs*, though this was also the title of one specific regiment. The others were the *Silaḥdars* (Ruler's Weapons Holders), *Ulufeciyân-i yemîn* (salaried men of the right), *Ulufeciyân-i yesar* (of the left), *Ǧurebâ-i yemîn* (non-Ottoman Muslims of the right) and *Ǧurebâ-i yesar* (of the left). Their numbers were small – a few hundred in each regiment – but they were superbly equipped and heavily armoured.

The Ottoman infantry were similarly divided into ordinary and elite formations. With the exception of camp followers, the lowest status Ottoman foot soldiers were the *Yaya*, who now served as an armed labour corps. The bulk of Ottoman foot soldiers consisted of the *azaps* or 'bachelors' recruited from the Muslim peasantry, a certain number being expected from a specified number of households. Though little more than irregulars they were effective enough as archers serving alongside the elite *Yeni Ceri* Janissaries. In fact, the numbers of *azaps* increased rapidly from the 1380s onwards, with many adopting the crossbow when serving at sea.

The most famous Ottoman infantry were, of course, the *Yeni Ceri*, or Janissaries. As the Ottoman conquests spread into the south-eastern Balkans in the 1360s they took numerous prisoners of war. Unlike their Christian foes, the Ottoman Turks rarely killed captives and a large number of young un-ransomed prisoners were considered a waste of military talent. The best were incorporated into the cavalry six regiments, and the Ottoman rulers also created an elite infantry regiment called the

The main mosque at Didimotihon in the far north-eastern corner of Greece was started by Murad I and completed by Bāyazîd in 1402. Didimotihon may briefly have been the first Ottoman capital in Europe. (Author's photograph)

Yeri Ceri or 'New Army'. It is unclear how many *ortas* or battalions existed at the time of Nicopolis but the best Janissaries did form one of Bāyazîd's ceremonial guard units, the *Solaks*, or *Rikabsolaklari*.

Vassal contingents varied in character and quality, those from Turkish Anatolian *beyliks* or small states tending to be unreliable. The *Muteferrikas* included the sons of senior Ottoman noblemen as well as vassal princes, but their presence at the Ottoman court was largely as hostages for their father's loyalty. The *Voynuqs* were Balkan Christian auxiliaries, many with their own *Jamaq* armed followers, while the smaller number of *Lagators* may have been senior *Voynuqs* – their name stemming from the Byzantine Greek *allagator* or member of a provincial military unit.

Where morale was concerned, the Anatolian Turkish attitude was summed up in a poem by Burhan al-Dîn, the religious judge of Erzinjan who died two years after the battle of Nicopolis: 'Thanks be to God it is now the day of heroes, the whole world sees this is an age of strife. From the land of the setting sun to the land where it rises, the man of love [meaning the mystical lover of God] flies in one fleeting breath.' Like the Western European knightly class, the Ottoman military elite were keen on winning fame in this world, as well as Paradise in the next, and their attitude to warfare is reflected in the *Iskander Nameh* written by Ahmedî a few years after Nicopolis:

The ruined upper tower of Curtea de Arges on the southern slopes of the Carpathian mountains.

'Those who've left a famous name never died,
  Those who've left no trace never lived.
Surely this is why you came to earth,
  That men should recall your worth.
May I not die! say you of noble birth?
  Strive then, that you leave a blessed name.'

According to another Turkish writer, Oruj, frontier warriors described themselves as 'Friends of strangers, blazing forth the way of Islam from the East to the West'. Nevertheless, the Islam of early Ottoman soldiers was hardly orthodox. Even a senior *imām* or religious leader of Bāyazîd's reign wrote a poem proclaiming the Prophets Muhammad and Jesus equal in status, though he was murdered by a fundamentalist not long after.

On the battlefield banners and military music played a major role in maintaining Ottoman morale, as they had done throughout Islamic history. Some flags were religious while others symbolised the presence of the ruler or indicated the chain of command in a clearer manner than was seen in European armies. As Konstantin Mihailovic wrote a generation after Nicopolis: 'One banner is white [the *Ak Sancak*], inscribed with gold letters, and that banner is supreme for it signifies that all the Sultan's power is there ... The second banner is red and this is the Court Cavalry's [the six Bölük Regiments]. The third banner is green and red. The fourth is red and gold, and these are the Janissary Infantry's'.

SERBIAN ARMIES

A military system resembling Western European feudalism reached its fullest development in parts of the Orthodox Christian Balkans during the 14th century. Generally speaking the western Balkans were under greater European feudal influence than was the east, the north more than the south. In most of the later 14th-century Slav-speaking Balkan countries, however, the land was dominated by *boyars* or great barons who had their own powerful military retinues.

Serbia fitted this pattern although the ruling prince's army was, at least theoretically, commanded by the *Great Voivode*, lesser *voivodes* and *Tisucnik* 'leaders of one thousand' while the term *Vitez* could be translated as 'knight'. Serbia's new-found wealth based on silver mines also permitted its rulers to import Italian arms and armour. Much of the military elite was supported by estates known as *pronijar*, from the original Byzantine Greek *pronoia*. The lesser Serbian military aristocracy was known as *Voynuj* (or *Wojnuq*) and they served as relatively heavily armoured cavalry. Their military organisation is unclear but the theoretical units of 50, 100 and 1000 men are likely to have had features in common with the late Byzantine system of *allagia* regiments. In addition to a quasi-feudal military elite and assorted mercenaries, the Serbian ruler could also call upon a general levy of free men comparable to the Great Army of Wallachia.

The little that is known about Serbian tactics suggests that they had features in common with those of the Bulgarians and Byzantines of the same period. According to the Byzantine Emperor Manuel II, writing around 1400, a member of the military aristocracy should know 'how to handle the bow and the spear and how to ride a horse' before the age of 16. Meanwhile in open battle both Serbian and Bulgarian cavalry tended to be placed ahead of a defensive infantry array.

Towers flanking the main gate on the landward side of Vidin Castle. (Author's photograph)

THE OPPOSING PLANS

CRUSADER INVASION PLANS

The idea that the Crusaders intended to march to Jerusalem is a myth. Nevertheless, the ultimate intentions of the Crusading army were never made clear. Similarly Sigismund is unlikely to have wanted an entirely defensive or static campaign as it was impossible to maintain a large medieval army in one spot for any length of time. He probably wanted a pre-emptive invasion of Bulgaria. Sigismund may also have preferred the army to march through Transylvania into Wallachia, confirming the shaky allegiance of both the Transylvanians and Wallachians.

The French and Burgundian commanders, fearing the Carpathian mountain passes, wanted to stay close to their Danubian supply convoy and may have hoped to separate Serbia from the Ottomans. Thereafter they probably envisaged a march across Bulgaria to capture the Ottoman capital of Edirne, saving the remnants of the Byzantine Empire and forcing the Ottomans back into Anatolia. If this was their intention their preparations made sense since Nicopolis was an ideal base for subsequent operations southwards.

Nevertheless, the Crusading army of 1396 was typical in lacking resources for a prolonged campaign. Its logistics also left much to be desired and its commanders largely ignored the advice of those with experience of fighting the Ottomans. Its failure at its first test resulted from military arrogance, ignorance of the enemy and the fact that the Crusaders faced one of the best commanders of the age – Yildirim Bãyazîd.

Balkan armour. ABOVE **Though sometimes believed to have been made much earlier, this one-piece iron helmet from Ozana might date from the late medieval period. (Provincial Museum, inv. 199, Kazanlik).** BELOW **The dating of this helmet from Berkasova is even more dubious. Said to be 6th-century, it is more likely 14th-, or even 15th-century. (Narodni Muzej, Belgrade; author's photograph)**

MORAVIA

POLAND

LITHUANIA

Brünn

Cracow

Lvov

GALICH VLADIMIR

AUSTRIA

Danube

Vienna

Pozsony

STYRIA

Graz

Kassa

Budapest

Crusader army leaves Budapest

Debrecen

HUNGARY

Kolozsvár

MOLDAVIA

Suceava

Dniestr

GOLDEN HORDE

Zágráb

Pécs

Danube supply fleet sails down river to Orşova

Szeged

Temesvár

Main Crusader marches overland to Orşova

Part of Crusader army marches through southern Transylvania into Wallachia to restore Mircea to the throne

Bilhorod (Moncastro)

Kiliya (Licostomo)

Brassó

Belgrade

Orşova

Supply fleet ferries main Crusader army over Danube to Orşova

Tirgovişte

WALLACHIA

BOSNIA

Zara

Spalato

Crusaders capture Vidin, early September 1396

Vidin

VIDIN

Orjahovo

Nicopolis

Girugiu

Danube

BLACK SEA

Nish

SERBIA

Crusaders raid territory around Vidin, early September 1396

Tarnovo

Varna

REPUBLIC OF RAGUSA

Sofia

Crusader fleet sails from Rhodes via the Dardanelles & Bosphorus to the mouth of the Danube, August 1896

Bari

NAPLES

Taranto

Skopje

Plovdiv

Maritsa

O T T O M A N

Edirne

Bāyazīd takes most of his army from the siege of Constantinople to Edirne, August 1396; siege of Constantinople reduced to a loose blockade

Constantinople

Local Rulers

Thessaloniki

Enez

Gallipoli

E M P I R E

Bursa

BYZANTINE EMPIRE

Izmir

DUCHY OF ATHENS

PRINCIPALITY OF ACHAIA

Athens

BYZANTINE EMPIRE

VENETIAN REPUBLIC

Rhodes

Crusader fleet sails from Rhodes via the Dardanelles & Bosphorus to the mouth of the Danube, August 1896

Crete

MEDITERRANEAN SEA

N

Legend:
- Venetian territory & colonies
- Genoese territory & colonies
- Poland (plus Galich-Vladimir)
- Moldavia
- Ottoman territory
- Ottoman vassals
- Knights of St. John
- Hungary
- Hungarian vassals
- Byzantine Empire

- Route of main Crusader army
- Route of Crusaders' Danube supply fleet
- Route of Crusader fleet
- Route of small Crusader force through Transylvania
- Possible route of part of Danube supply fleet through Iron Gates to Vidin
- Presumed communications with Crusader fleet at the mouth of the Danube
- Ottoman palace army reduces siege of Constantinople and marches to Edirne

0   100 miles
0   200 km

THE OTTOMAN DEFENCE PLAN

Bãyazîd's strategy before the Crusade had been to consolidate his control over Bulgaria, without which the Ottoman position in Europe was untenable. The only large fortified town on the northern Danube frontier was Vidin, which was in vassal Bulgarian rather than Ottoman territory. Other strong points along the Danube were smaller, though some, like Nicopolis, commanded important crossing points over this strategically vital river.

Bãyazîd had, in fact, made Nicopolis the centre of Ottoman power in this region, entrusting it to an experienced veteran named Doğan Beg. Nevertheless, the Ottomans disliked committing good troops to garrison duties and instead used their Balkan auxiliaries or vassals to hold fortified places. This meant that the bulk of the Ottoman army was available for major campaigns, even at short notice.

Once the Crusaders invaded Ottoman territory, Doğan Beg was ordered to resist to the last. The importance Bãyazîd gave to the Nicopolis garrison may even indicate that he knew his enemies' intentions. Furthermore the campaign took place when the Ottomans' horses had been fattened by a recent harvest and much of the army was already assembled for the siege of Constantinople. Even the bloody conqueror Tîmur-i Lang was focused elsewhere. The result was, of course, a complete victory.

'The Betrayal', on a wall painting, Transylvanian 1400–1420. (*in situ*, Lutheran Church, Medias; author's photograph)

ASSEMBLING THE CRUSADING ARMY

A Burgundian *Ordnance,* or official proclamation, fixed Dijon as the place where the Franco-Burgundian Crusaders should assemble by 20 April 1396. Other *Ordnances* set out rules by which the army would be organised, supplied and disciplined. In battle 'The Count [of Nevers] and his company always claim the *avant garde*', which would lead to disaster at Nicopolis. Other disciplinary regulations shed light on prevailing attitudes. For example, a nobleman causing disruption could lose his horse and harness, whereas a non-noble drawing a knife in a quarrel would lose a hand and anyone caught stealing would lose an ear.

Many such documents survive and they give an impression of what the army was really like. It was formed around the military household or

Painted statuette of Hüglin von Schoenegg, Marshal of the Duchy of Spoleto, *c.*1380. (Historisches Museum, Basel)

33

Hôtel of the Count of Nevers, which was effectively an army within an army. At the start of the campaign this *Hôtel* was a coherent military structure consisting of 108 knights, 107 squires, 12 archers and 22 crossbowmen. The rest of the Franco-Burgundian contingent largely consisted of the *hôtels* of other senior noblemen. Boucicault, for example, brought along 15 knights and 70 'gentlemen'.

The amount of paperwork dedicated to banners shows how important they were. The Duke of Burgundy had no less than 16 made for his son, Count John of Nevers, representing the Duke's close association with the Crusade as well as the expedition's supposedly spiritual purpose. Eight bore the image of the Virgin Mary, the patron of Crusaders, four white and four blue, while eight bore the arms of Burgundy. Philippe de Mussy was chosen as standard-bearer with an escort of three senior knights (Jacques de Courtiambles, Jean de Blaisy and Damas de Buxeul) while a squire named Jean de Gruuthuse carried the Count's own pennon with an escort of two squires (Philippot de Nanton and Huguenin de Lugny). The Count's escort consisted of six knights from his *Hôtel* (Guillaume de Mello, Jean de Blaisy, who escorted the standard-bearer, Jean de Sainte-Croix, Hélion de Naillac – brother of Philibert de Naillac – Guillaume de Vienne and Geoffrey de Charny). Officers in charge of food and other supplies were also selected, including the *maître d'hôtel*, *écuyer panetier*, *écuyer échanson*, two *écuyers de cuisine*, a butcher and a *poulailler*.

THE MARCH TO NICOPOLIS

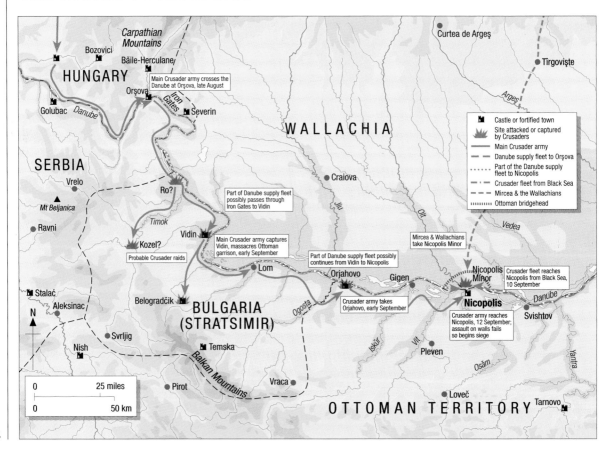

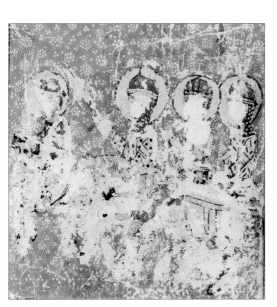

Another damaged manuscript illustration from the *Iskander Nameh*. The horsemen have pointed helmets, two with mail aventails, but the man in the centre also wields a Western European sword of a type not normally seen in the Islamic world. (*Iskander Nameh*, Bib. Nat., Ms. Turc. 309, f.296r, Paris)

Most leaders were drawn from the Duke of Burgundy's *Hôtel* and the Council selected to advise the young Count of Nevers consisted of Philippe de Bar, Admirale Jean de Vienne, Guy de la Trémoille, Guillaume de la Trémoille and Oudart de Chaseron. Other men summoned when required included: Jaques de Bourbon, the Comte de la Marche; Henri de Bar; Philippe d'Artois, the Constable of France; the Comte d'Eu and Marshal Boucicault. Enguerrand de Coucy arrived from Italy shortly before the expedition set out, and, flattered by the Duke and Duchess of Burgundy as the most experienced knight in France, also agreed to join the Crusade. A third group of high-ranking Burgundian knights was also occasionally consulted: Henri de Montbéliard, Henri de Châlon, Guillaume de Vienne, Jean de Châlons, Jacques de Vienne, Guillaume de Mello, Geoffrey de Charny, Jean de Blaisy, Jean de Trie and Hélion de Naillac – one-time chamberlain of the Duke of Burgundy. Several of these men also formed one of the banner escorts.

The Count of Nevers' *Hôtel* included 35 men with experience of Crusading warfare, but all save one had only campaigned in the Baltic or North Africa. Only Jeanne de Vienne had personal experience of the Ottoman Turks, having been with the Green Count of Savoy's expedition in 1366. Of course other men outside the *Hôtel* had not only fought against the Ottomans, but some had even been mercenaries in Ottoman service.

Meanwhile small Crusading contingents assembled in Germany, where one of the first to take the Cross was Count Palatine Ruprecht Pipan, eldest son of Duke Robert III of Bavaria. Others included one of the three Counts of Katznellenbogen, Count Herman II of Cilly, Burgrave John III of Nuremberg and other knights from Bavaria, Meissen, Thuringia, Saxony, Hesse, the Rhineland, Swabia, Alsace, Steiermark and Luxembourg. Some Englishmen are said to have accompanied the Crusade, perhaps led by the Earl of Huntingdon. A small contingent arrived from Aragon in Spain, as did several Polish knights.

But there was also criticism of this Crusade. The lifelong Crusading propagandist Philippe de Mézières maintained that things were being done the wrong way. Aged almost seventy and living in the Convent of the Celestines in Paris, Philippe fulminated against those who organised the Crusade. They had ignored his advice and were morally unprepared because, he believed, the knights were being drawn east by 'Vain Madame Ambition, one of the Mightiest Ladies in the World'. It would, he proclaimed, end in disaster.

At Dijon the assembled Franco-Burgundian Crusaders were given four months' advance on their wages while 133 members of the Count of Nevers' *Hôtel* were issued with bright green liveries. A few days after 20 April 1396 the Franco-Burgundian Crusaders set out. Enguerrand de Coucy, Henri de Bar and a smaller French party may already have been heading for Milan and Venice. On 30 April Count John of Nevers joined his troops, who had by now reached Montbéliard, and together they began their march east.

Ruins of the small medieval church of Sts. Peter and Paul beneath the north-western corner of the upper town of Nicopolis. (Author's photograph)

In March, Hérédia, the Grand Master of the Hospitallers, had died at Rhodes, whereupon the Grand Chapter elected Philibert de Naillac as his successor. Whether he had yet arrived from France is unclear but he was soon arming a squadron of Hospitaller galleys, ready to join ships from Venice, Genoese Chios and Mitilene (modern Lesvos) as planned.

The first stage of the Crusaders' march to Vienna went smoothly. On 11 May the city council of Regensburg was asked for boats to carry supplies down the Danube. German forces under Count Palatine Ruprecht and the Count of Katznellenbogen also joined the French and Burgundians at Regensburg. On 21 May the Franco-Burgundian vanguard under D'Eu and Boucicault reached Vienna, followed three days later by the main force. There they were royally entertained by the Duke of

The Orta Hamam or 'Regimental Bathhouse' in Bolu was built during the reign of Bāyazîd in the late 14th century. (Author's photograph)

The tomb of Gāzî Evrenos Beg in his mausoleum at Yiannitsa in northern Greece. (photograph, The 11th Ephorate of Byzantine Antiquities, Veroia)

Austria, though some of the priests accompanying the army were already complaining about the troops' immorality.

Meanwhile the Sire de Coucy and his smaller party reached Milan, where their mission to mollify Giangaleazzo Visconti failed. He was furious at losing control over Genoa and was also upset by the way his daughter Valentina had been treated at the French court. Not the least bit daunted, De Coucy and De Bar travelled on to Venice, where records indicate that they took ship to Senj on the Hungarian-ruled Dalmatian coast. From there De Coucy's party probably travelled direct to Budapest, where they found that other Crusader units had already arrived, including those under the Bastard of Savoy, some Bohemians, perhaps some Teutonic Knights and some Poles. The Hungarians were also gathering, along with some Wallachians under the *voivode* Mircea.

A river fleet of 70 ships and barges also sailed down the Danube from Vienna to Buda, followed by the main Crusader army, which arrived late in July. The size of the army that eventually encamped outside Budapest led King Sigismund to write that: 'Their lances could have upheld the sky from falling'. Nevertheless, their true numbers have been the subject of prolonged debate. In fact the Crusaders probably numbered some 16,000 men. Traditional Turkish sources give the number of Ottoman troops as 10,000 but when their Balkans vassals were included they may have numbered around 15,000. One thing is clear, the forces that eventually faced each other outside Nicopolis were similar in number.

The Danube looking upstream from the old town of Nicopolis. On the left are the hills of Bulgaria, on the right the flat plain of Wallachia. (Author's photograph)

THE INVASION

The strategy pursued by the Crusaders was eventually agreed in Budapest. Sigismund had expected an Ottoman invasion but this never materialised and Hungarian reconnaissance found no evidence of major Ottoman forces near the frontiers. Thereupon the French and Burgundians are said to have declared Bāyazîd a coward who feared to face them and insisted on an immediate offensive to which Sigismund reluctantly agreed. In reality some sort of expedition into the Balkans must already have been envisaged since a Crusader fleet was assembling in the Black Sea.

Nicolas de Gara, the Constable of Hungary, led the vanguard down the left bank of the Danube, followed by the French and Burgundians with King Sigismund and the main Hungarian force in the rear. Meanwhile a convoy of supply vessels sailed down the river. At Orsova, a few kilometres upstream from the narrow rushing defile of the Iron Gates, the army assembled to cross the Danube. On one side rose the southern Carpathian Mountains, on the other the broken and hilly terrain of eastern Serbia. It took eight days to ferry the troops across the Danube and almost at once the French and Burgundians started ill-treating the local Orthodox Christian population. They were, of course, in Ottoman vassal territory though to the Hungarians this territory rightly owed allegiance to them. Priests and friars pleaded for better behaviour but, as one cleric from St. Denis recalled: 'They might as well

The so-called Clock Tower in Edirne is almost all that remains of the city's Romano-Byzantine fortifications. Edirne was the capital of the Ottoman state at the time of Nicopolis. (Author's photograph)

38

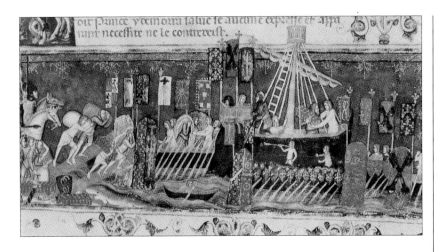

have talked to a deaf ass.' Franco-Burgundian overconfidence may also have accounted for a lack of precautions during the next stage of the march to Vidin. It is not clear whether the river supply fleet sailed beyond the Iron Gates, though the number of small vessels later reported at Nicopolis suggests that some did so.

Part of the Hungarian army had taken a different route through Transylvania to cross the Carpathians into Wallachia. Apart from gathering Transylvanian contingents they seem to have expelled Mircea's pro-Ottoman rival Vlad and driven a small Ottoman garrison from Nicopolis Minor. It would also seem likely that, having regained control of Wallachia, Mircea contacted the Crusader fleet anchored near the mouth of the Danube. The exact location of the fleet is unknown, though the Genoese colonial outpost of Killia is probable. Forty-four vessels under the overall command of the famous Venetian admiral Thomas Mocenigo had left Rhodes in August and on 29 or 30 August all or part of this armada sailed up the Danube.

According to Froissart the invaders attacked several places after crossing the river including a castle, perhaps Belogradcik, which resisted until the Crusader army marched on to Nicopolis. One of the brothers in command of this fort then went to warn Bāyazîd of the invasion. This may be true, though the Ottoman ruler had plenty of other warnings.

Vidin was the capital of a small Bulgarian principality, a vassal of the Ottoman state, but had also been held by the Hungarians in the 1360s. Its castle was strong and its moat could apparently be filled from the Danube. But when the Crusader army arrived early in September the Bulgarian ruler John Strachimir opened the city gates. The tiny Ottoman garrison, reportedly commanded by a 'Greek Christian' or *Voynuq* auxiliary leader, was promptly massacred and replaced by 200–300 invaders. This was the Crusaders' first clash of arms and so the Count of Nevers and 300 men were ceremoniously knighted on the 'field of honour'.

Orjahovo was a strongly fortified town overlooking the Danube, reportedly with a double wall, of which nothing remains. It guarded an important ferry point and was strongly garrisoned because this was the frontier of Ottoman rather than vassal territory. Hoping to take the garrison by surprise, a band of 500 French and Burgundians led by the Constable d'Eu and Marshal Boucicault marched through the night to launch a dawn attack without waiting for Hungarian support. However, the locals destroyed the bridge over the moat and the assault failed. Several further attacks were thrown back until the arrival of the Hungarians convinced the defenders that they should surrender. The Ottoman commander sent a delegation to the Crusader camp, offering to lay down his arms in return for the garrison's lives. Sigismund would have granted this request but the other Crusaders claimed that their men had already scaled the walls and had the right of conquest. The result was another massacre of both Muslims and Orthodox Christians, though the Crusaders kept many of the wealthier citizens, and perhaps the garrison, prisoner in the hope of earning ransoms. Once again the Hungarians felt that their King had been insulted.

Meanwhile the Venetian, Genoese and Hospitaller ships made their way upstream; a journey of 12 days along a broad river which posed no problems for medieval ships. The Danube was about one kilometre wide at Nicopolis though the islands and marshes downstream stretched further. The fleet probably arrived on 10 September and anchored out of arrow-range until the main army arrived two days later.

The medieval gate of the Hisar Kapija or Citadel of Plovdiv. (Author's photograph)

The Shipka Pass through the Balkan Mountains. Bāyazīd and Stefan Lazarevic led their troops though here before linking up at Tarnovo. (Author's photograph)

Nicopolis stood on a high bluff overlooking the Danube. It was an important river port and ferry location, and lay close to the rivers Olt (leading northwards across Wallachia almost to Transylvania) and Osâm, whose valley led towards central Bulgaria. Nicopolis was, in fact, one of the most strategic positions on the lower Danube. It was also the strongest place the invaders had so far faced. Its fortifications had recently been strengthened and its large, well-supplied garrison was commanded by a highly experienced officer, Doğan Beg.

The Franco-Burgundian contingent in the vanguard established their camp facing the citadel while Sigismund and his Hungarians made camp facing the town. The defences were high on cliffs on several sides, but to the south-east the land ahead of the walls was relatively level though cut up by ravines. Nevertheless, the Franco-Burgundians made scaling ladders while the Hungarians dug two large mines towards the wall. Both tactics failed and later chroniclers complained of the Crusaders' lack of machines to batter the walls. This remains something of a mystery. Nothing was brought overland but it is unlikely that the Crusaders foresaw no need for siege engines. Perhaps such equipment remained aboard the ships or perhaps Nicopolis had such a strong natural position that the Crusader commanders decided to blockade in the hope of drawing Bāyazîd into a major battle. This was, of course, a common strategy and eventually the garrison would be starved into surrender while the Crusaders could be supplied by boat from friendly Wallachian territory.

Nor was there news of Bāyazîd coming to relieve the defenders, though the idea that the Crusaders were so overconfident that they neglected to send out scouting parties is almost certainly a myth, promoted by those explaining the defeat of a Christian army as a result of its own sins. Nevertheless, food from Wallachia must have limited the need for foraging far into unfriendly territory to the south. Pious chroniclers also exaggerated the decline of morals within the Crusader camp. On the other hand tension between the Hungarians and the Franco-Burgundians clearly increased while the Orthodox Wallachians must have been disturbed by Crusader behaviour towards the local Orthodox population, many of whom were probably Vlachs. Yet it was the unjustified confidence of the Crusader army that struck later chroniclers. Men who dared suggest that Bāyazîd was coming are said to have had their ears chopped off as 'rumour mongers'. For their part the Ottoman garrison defended themselves so effectively that once the siege was lifted their commander, Doğan Beg, was given the title of _Shujā al-Din_ or 'Hero of the Faith'.

The _Khwaju Kirmani_ manuscript, illustrated in Baghdad in 1396, shows the most advanced arms and armour used in the Islamic Middle East at the time of the Nicopolis Crusade. (Brit. Lib., Ms. Add. 18113, London)

BÃYAZÎD'S RESPONSE

Bãyazîd and the best of his army were besieging Constantinople when the Crusader army invaded. Ottoman intelligence services were as good as those of their Islamic predecessors and Bãyazîd may even have lifted the siege, burning any machinery that could not be easily moved, when the Crusaders left Budapest. The passage of a Crusader fleet through the Dardanelles and Bosphorus could hardly be hidden, and the fact that these vessels made no attempt to stop Ottoman troops from crossing into the Balkans suggests that the majority were already there. Bãyazîd is also said to have been gathering his forces near Edirne when a spy brought him a copy of a letter from the Byzantine Emperor Manuel to Sigismund of Hungary, declaring: 'Why do you delay? The Turks are preparing for you, prepare yourself!'

Information from the Ottoman side of the campaign is scarce, though the Byzantine chronicler Dukas stated that: 'Bãyazîd, who had been informed many days earlier of the gathering of the nations from the west, assembled his entire army from the east and west and, further augmented by troops who were laying siege to Constantinople, led them in person'. According to Ottoman chroniclers Bãyazîd sent Gãzî Evrenos Beg ahead with an advance guard of light cavalry, presumably to watch enemy movements, while a loose blockade was maintained around Constantinople. Perhaps this was why the Byzantines were unable to take part in naval operations.

Bãyazîd also ordered forces in the Balkans not to attack the Crusaders but to assemble between Edirne and Plovdiv. A formidable army gathered rapidly, provincial cavalry forming beneath the banners of their *Sancak Begs* then riding to the main assembly point while others remain to protect their home territory. Bãyazîd was naturally in overall command while his young sons were nominally in charge of Rumelian and Anatolian provincial contingents, supervised by the old and reliable Vizier Qara Tîmurtãsh Beg. Vassal contingents assembled around Plovdiv, with the Serbs under Stefan Lazarevic arriving via Sofia. The war-ravaged condition of the land may have accounted for the fact that the assembly area was spread out along the Marica river. The assembly area between Edirne and Plovdiv was also well south of Crusader patrols.

In later years it took an Ottoman army six weeks to assemble before moving off, but the speed of Bãyazîd's mobilisation and his reliance on a relatively small force clearly caught the Crusaders by surprise. In 1484 it took a larger Ottoman army, with a siege train, three weeks to get from Edirne across the Danube. In 1396 Bãyazîd seemingly moved faster.

'St. Merkurios' on an early 14th-century Macedonian wall painting. (*in situ* Church of St. Klement, Ohrid)

The *Dānishmandnāme*, one of the earliest pieces of Ottoman Turkish literature dating from the 1360s, described such an army setting out. Its senior men took their robes of honour and horses, as well as religious banners, flags associated with earlier heroes, large drums and pairs of small gilded drums. The Ottoman army's normal order of march was led by a scouting party consisting of the *akincis*, probably under Gāzî Evrenos Beg, followed by a mounted 'pioneer corps' of *müsellems* to ensure that roads, bridges and passes were in good repair. Next came a vanguard of

BĀYAZÎD STRIKES BACK

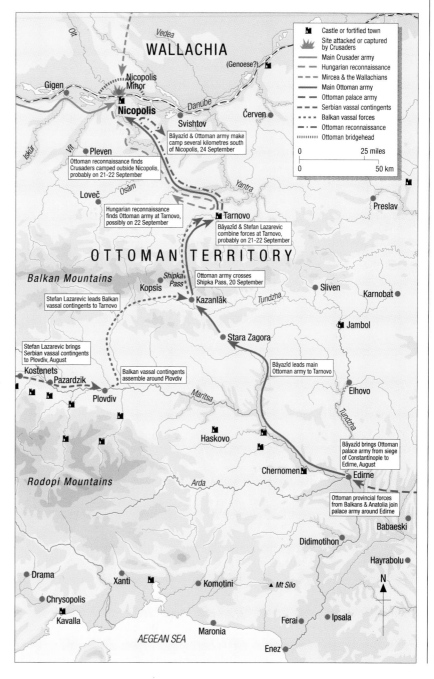

Castle or fortified town
Site attacked or captured by Crusaders
Main Crusader army
Hungarian reconnaissance
Mircea & the Wallachians
Main Ottoman army
Ottoman palace army
Serbian vassal contingents
Balkan vassal forces
Ottoman reconnaissance
Ottoman bridgehead

0   25 miles
0   50 km

WALLACHIA

(Genoese?)

Vedea
Olt
Gigen
Nicopolis Minor
Nicopolis
Danube
Svishtov
Červen
Iskŭr
Vit
Pleven
Osăm
Yantra
Loveč
Preslav
Tarnovo
OTTOMAN TERRITORY
Balkan Mountains
Shipka Pass
Kopsis
Kazanlăk
Sliven
Karnobat
Stefan Lazarevic leads Balkan vassal contingents to Tarnovo
Tundzha
Jambol
Stara Zagora
Kostenets
Pazardzik
Balkan vassal contingents assemble around Plovdiv
Plovdiv
Maritsa
Elhovo
Haskovo
Tundzha
Chernomen
Edirne
Rodopi Mountains
Arda
Babaeski
Didimotihon
Hayrabolu
Drama
Xanti
Komotini
Mt Silo
N
Chrysopolis
Kavalla
Ferai
Ipsala
Maronia
AEGEAN SEA
Enez

Bāyazîd & Ottoman army make camp several kilometres south of Nicopolis, 24 September

Ottoman reconnaissance finds Crusaders camped outside Nicopolis, probably on 21-22 September

Hungarian reconnaissance finds Ottoman army at Tarnovo, possibly on 22 September

Bāyazîd & Stefan Lazarevic combine forces at Tarnovo, probably on 21-22 September

Ottoman army crosses Shipka Pass, 20 September

Stefan Lazarevic brings Serbian vassal contingents to Plovdiv, August

Bāyazîd leads main Ottoman army to Tarnovo

Bāyazîd brings Ottoman palace army from siege of Constantinople to Edirne, August

Ottoman provincial forces from Balkans & Anatolia join palace army around Edirne

The medieval citadel of Tarnovo, dominated by the 13th-century Patriarchate Church. (Author's photograph)

elite cavalry, followed by the main force of infantry, the ruler's household cavalry, armourers and specialist troops. The flanks were protected by provincial *sipahî* cavalry while a baggage train brought up the rear.

The main Ottoman army headed directly from Edirne to Tarnovo while the Serbians marched from Plovdiv, both forces crossing the rugged Balkan range via the Shipka Pass on 20 and 21 September. They then linked up at Tarnovo on the 21st or 22nd where the Ottoman army was finally found by a Hungarian reconnaissance under John of Maroth, the experienced *ban* of the area around Belgrade. Meanwhile Ottoman reconnaissance patrols found the Crusader camp outside Nicopolis.

The Ottomans do not seem to have been challenged before they reached Nicopolis and, on 24 September, Bāyazîd established his camp on a hill several kilometres south of the town. A Turkish version of the *Varqa ve Gülşāh* romance written by Yusuf-i Meddāh in the late

A narrow neck of land spans the valley between the site of the Citadel of Nicopolis, seen here, and hills to the east. (Author's photograph)

This splendid German panel painting of the Crucifixion dates from the start of the 15th century. (*in situ* Erfurt Cathedral; author's photograph)

14th century adds colourful details of making camp: 'Drum and fife and trumpet were played. There were horse-tail emblems, lances, flags and banners topped with moons. All the army, rank upon rank, troop after troop, wore iron armour on his lower and upper body. All dismounted from their horses. They camped opposite the enemy, set up their tents, the tent-ropes interwoven, they covered the face of the sun. They set up the chief's tent, and other tents and pavilions'.

Ottoman sources maintain that Bāyazîd reached the walls of Nicopolis, probably at night, and spoke with Doğan Beg, but he is unlikely to have delivered additional supplies. In fact the Ottoman chronicler Nesri says that these were not needed; the garrison commander telling Bāyazîd that: 'Our supplies are plentiful, and now that the Sultan is here we shall not be defeated,' to which Bāyazîd supposedly replied: 'Hang on bravely, I will look after you. You shall see that I will be here like a flash of lightning!'

Bāyazîd now decided to adopt traditional Islamic tactics and make the enemy attack him. Equally clearly the Crusaders were not surprised in their camp by the Ottomans. Instead the Ottomans erected field fortifications on ground of their own choosing. According to late 14th-century Mamluk military manuals these should have consisted of trenches and a palisade with gaps defended by infantry archers and cavalry. European accounts of Nicopolis describe a hedge of sharpened stakes forming the equivalent of a palisade but make no mention of a ditch, though later Ottoman armies did use entrenchments.

The Crusaders now found themselves with an enemy army on one side, an enemy garrison behind them, and no strong base to fall back upon. The Danube also lay between them and Wallachia. If defeated the Crusaders would be trapped and this fact, as well as the traditionally offensive tactics of the French and Burgundians, necessitated their taking the offensive.

Reconnaissance of the area was carried out on 24 September, if not earlier, by Mircea and his Wallachians plus some Germans, and by De Coucy and other Crusaders. Neither are mentioned in Ottoman sources while European chronicles are confused or exaggerated. The first was probably that by Mircea. Sigismund allowed him to take '1000 men for the purpose of looking at the winds, and he returned to the king and told him that he ... had seen 20 banners and there were 10,000 men under each banner, and each banner was separate from the others'. In other words the Ottoman array consisted of 20 units. De Coucy's supposed 'raid' is more of a problem, though it probably clashed with Gâzî Evrenos Beg's *akincis*. Its leaders included Reynaud de Roye, Jean de Saimpy, the Chamberlain of Burgundy, the Châtelain de Beauvais and the Sire de Montcavrel. They had a detachment of 500 men-at-arms and

DE COUCY'S RAID: 24 SEPTEMBER

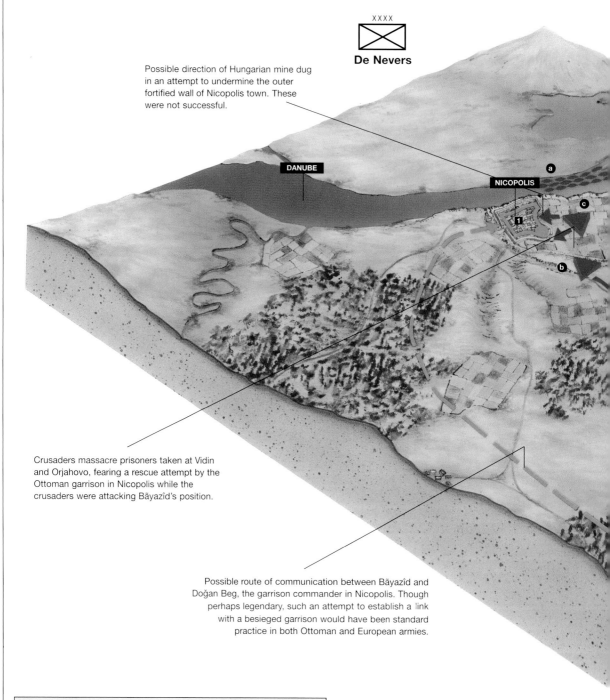

XXXX
De Nevers

Possible direction of Hungarian mine dug in an attempt to undermine the outer fortified wall of Nicopolis town. These were not successful.

DANUBE

NICOPOLIS

Crusaders massacre prisoners taken at Vidin and Orjahovo, fearing a rescue attempt by the Ottoman garrison in Nicopolis while the crusaders were attacking Bāyazīd's position.

Possible route of communication between Bāyazīd and Doğan Beg, the garrison commander in Nicopolis. Though perhaps legendary, such an attempt to establish a link with a besieged garrison would have been standard practice in both Ottoman and European armies.

CRUSADER UNITS	OTTOMAN UNITS
a Crusader fleet anchored near north bank of Danube.	**1** Ottoman garrison in Nicopolis, commanded by Doğan Beg.
b Franco-Burgundian encampment, under Count of Nevers.	**2** Ottoman army under Bāyazīd.
c Hungarian encampment plus smaller contingents, under King Sigismund.	**3** *Akincis* as advance guard.
d De Coucy's Forces.	

XXXX

Sigismund

Crusader army re-supplied from friendly territory in Wallachia across the Danube, using boats from the Crusader fleet. Although such a supply system is not mentioned in the sources, it must have taken place and would have lessened the need for foraging expeditions into the hostile territory outside Nicopolis

Probable direction of the large scale reconnaissance by Mircea and the Wallachians. Also the probable route of a supposed raid by the Sire de Coucy, which may, in reality, have formed part of Mircea's reconnaissance.

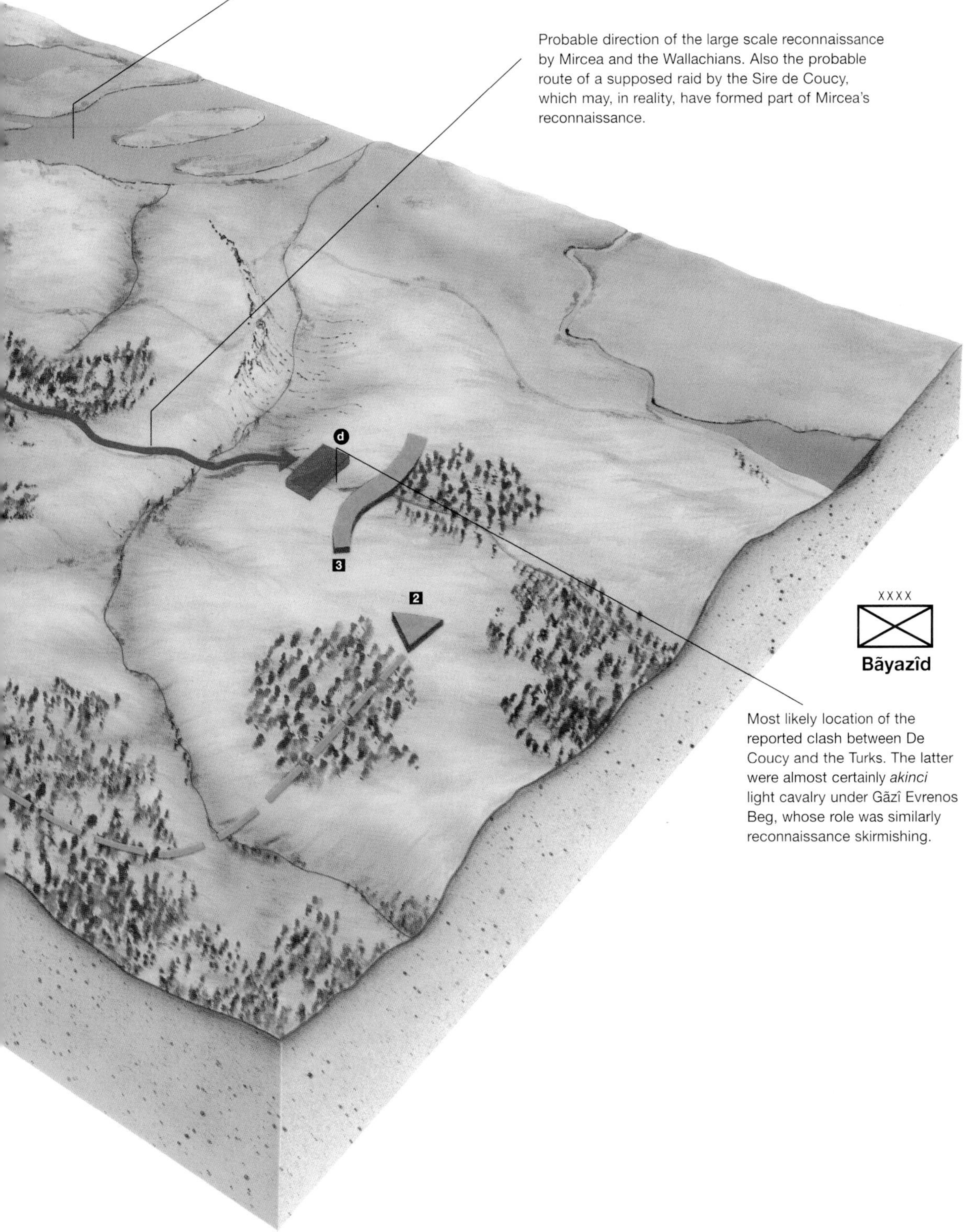

d

3

2

XXXX

Bãyazîd

Most likely location of the reported clash between De Coucy and the Turks. The latter were almost certainly *akinci* light cavalry under Gāzî Evrenos Beg, whose role was similarly reconnaissance skirmishing.

a similar number of mounted crossbowmen or archers, in the latter case possibly Wallachians, plus Hungarian guides. According to Froissart a far larger force of Turks was found guarding a 'pass' but De Coucy, Froissart's hero and benefactor, prepared a counter-ambush. Two hundred French horsemen drew the Turks into pursuit, whereupon the rest of the Crusaders charged shouting 'Our Lady be with the Sire de Coucy', virtually annihilating the Turks. Exaggerated as this account is, it might reflect the tactical influence of De Coucy's Wallachian friends, he being almost the only French nobleman who got on well with Mircea. De Coucy's 'raid' may, indeed, have been part of the larger reconnaissance by Mircea.

Also on 24 September, the Crusaders, perhaps fearing a rescue sortie by the garrison in Nicopolis, massacred thousands of prisoners from Orjahovo. Such drastic action was common enough on Western European battlefields, but it was new to the Ottomans. The Crusaders also had no time to bury the dead and this would ultimately cost them dear.

THE BATTLE

The battle of Nicopolis was fought in Monday 25 September 1396 AD on open ground not far from the walls of the town. Its precise location is, however, a matter of debate. Neither of the two most likely places fit all of the details in all of the sources. The battlefield selected for this interpretation is on a spur of land fronted by a deep valley almost midway between Nicopolis and the modern village of Belavoda. There is no longer a road as this point though there is an agricultural track leading from a probable gate in the medieval walls of Nicopolis, across a ford and joining a road which leads to Tarnovo via the Yantra valley.

Bāyazîd was on slightly higher ground than the plateau south-east of Nicopolis and used natural features to secure his position. His left flank was close to a wood while his right flank was protected by broken ground beyond which steep slopes led down to marshes along the Danube. Most important of all there was a narrow wooden ravine to his front.

The Ottoman array was relatively straightforward and fully within 14th-century Anatolian Turkish military traditions. These habitually placed infantry archers ahead of the main cavalry element, which was itself divided into a larger centre with smaller wings which could be thrust forwards, giving the whole array a crescent formation. As was also traditional, Balkan or Rumelian cavalry were placed on the right wing because this battle was on European soil. Anatolian cavalry was on the left. Infantry were in the centre protected by a deep thicket of sharpened wooden stakes. The few existing Janissary *ortas* were probably amongst the ordinary *azap* foot soldiers rather than being held back with Bāyazîd's household cavalry corps. In front of the stakes were light cavalry *akincis*, who were intended to draw the enemy forward against the main field defences and expose them to cavalry flank attacks.

Meanwhile Bāyazîd was some distance to the rear behind the brow of the hill, surrounded by his personal guard and presumably with household regiments to right and left. To one side of the Ottoman household division, probably the left, was the Serbian vassal contingent under Stefan Lazarevic. Further details recorded in the Ottoman *Niğbolu zafer-nâmesi'ne* (Eulogy for the Nicopolis Victory) indicate that the Rumelian provincial cavalry was commanded by Bāyazîd's son, Süleyman Çeleb, supported by Ali Paşa Cāndārli and the Rumelian *Beglerbegs* Fîrûz,

A wooden mosque with a wooden minaret in the old town of Nicopolis. (Author's photograph)

Malkoç and Tîmurtāsh (not to be confused with Qara Tîmurtāsh pasa). The Anatolian provincial cavalry was commanded by another of Bāyazīd's sons, Mustafa Çelebî, supported by the Anatolian *Beglerbeg* Qara Tîmurtāsh Pasa and including Turkish vassal contingents, mostly from ex-Qaramānian territory, commanded by Mehmed Beg, Turhan Beg, Beşir Beg and Tâhir Beg. Bāyazīd planned to draw the Crusaders into an assault and then hit them in the flanks while they were fighting his infantry. However, the Franco-Burgundians broke through the Ottoman infantry more quickly than expected and they also attacked so precipitously that the Crusader army was effectively divided into two parts.

With the exception of King Sigismund's Wallachian and Transylvanian vassals, the morale of both armies was high, but when it came to discipline things were different. Like most Western European armies, the Crusaders were not specifically trained to cope with a reversal. The Ottomans were, and as a result they did not run away when beaten. Instead they re-formed behind their original positions. Nor did the Crusader army rush head-long into battle 'hot with wine and courage' as has been suggested. Its leaders had hurried from their evening banquet to an acrimonious discussion the previous evening, but the morrow's battle array had been agreed. Sigismund advised caution and, supported by De Coucy, wanted to discover whether Bāyazīd was going to attack. He also wanted to send Transylvanian and Wallachian light cavalry to clear the field of *akincis*. Mircea accepted this role and may have volunteered to open the assault since he had some claim to this territory. The French and Burgundian men-at-arms would then attack the

'Alexander, his Persian advisors and his army' in a 14th-century Byzantine manuscript. (*Codex of Alexander the Great*, Library of S. Giorgio dei Greci, Venice)

Ottoman main force, supported by the Hungarians and other Crusaders. Many of the Franco-Burgundian leaders were furious at the idea of entering battle behind those they regarded as peasants, and the Count d'Eu is even said to have declared: 'Yes, yes, the King of Hungary wants to have the flowers of the day and the honour!'

Sigismund gave way and the following morning the Franco-Burgundians took up their position at the front of the army. Behind them, along a broader front, were the Hungarians, Germans, Hospitallers, and probably Bohemians and Poles. On the right were the Transylvanians led by Laczkovic and on the left were the Wallachians led

Hungarian knights on a late 14th-century wall painting of the Legend of Prince Ladislas. (*in situ* Church, Liptovsky Ondrej; photograph Statny ustav pamiatkovej starostlivosti, Bratislava)

by Mircea. This meant that the Crusaders' left flank rested near the slope leading down to the Danube while their right flank was not far from the head of two ravines which ran beneath the western wall of Nicopolis.

Early on the morning of 25 September, Sigismund sent his Grand Marshal to urge his allies not to advance too hastily from what was a good defensive position. The Count of Nevers now summoned his advisors. De Coucy agreed with Sigismund's advice, but D'Eu seized a banner of the Virgin and shouted: 'Forward in the name of God and St. George, today you shall see me a valorous knight'. The experienced De Coucy was horrified and turned to the Admiral de Vienne, who, perhaps with a Gallic shrug, replied: 'When truth and reason cannot be heard, then must arrogance rule'. Still they advised waiting for the Hungarians but D'Eu insisted on an immediate advance. Doubts concerning men's courage were exchanged and no one wanted to be shamed, so the attack was launched. D'Eu commanded the van, with the Count of Nevers, De Coucy and the main body close behind. Knights, squires and a small number of mounted infantry moved forward together, along with some German and other Crusaders including a few Wallachians.

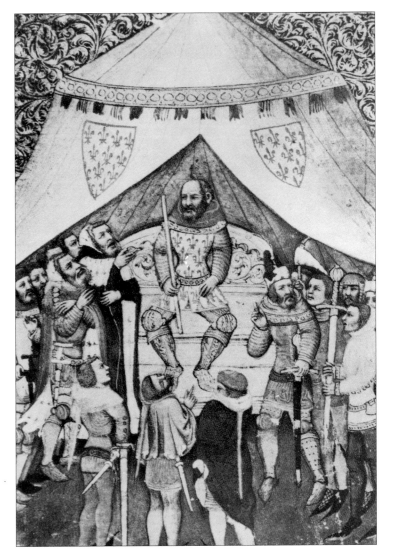

An army commander in his tent with his advisors, in a miniature painted by Niccolo da Bologna in 1373. (*De Bello Pharsalico*, Bib. Trivulziana, Ms. 691, f.86v, Milan)

The only Ottoman troops visible to Crusader scouting parties were light cavalry *akincis* on the slope of a hill beyond a narrow, wooded ravine. They are said to have obscured the thicket of sharpened stakes and Ottoman infantry beyond. Most probably the Crusader scouts skirmished with *akincis* on the plateau, breaking through onto the hillside beyond. Bāyazīd's household division and the Serbs were certainly obscured by the rounded shape of the hill.

Perhaps believing the European myth that Turkish armies consisted of lightly equipped horsemen, the Franco-Burgundian contingent moved forward towards the edge of the plateau without informing Sigismund. They now found the ground sloping down towards a dry stream bed with dense undergrowth and trees. It was not the function of *akincis* to confront a mass of heavily armoured horsemen and any fighting would have been little more than skirmishing. European chronicles maintain that this ill-equipped Ottoman light cavalry scattered and thus exposed the

THE MAIN ASSAULT: 25 SEPTEMBE

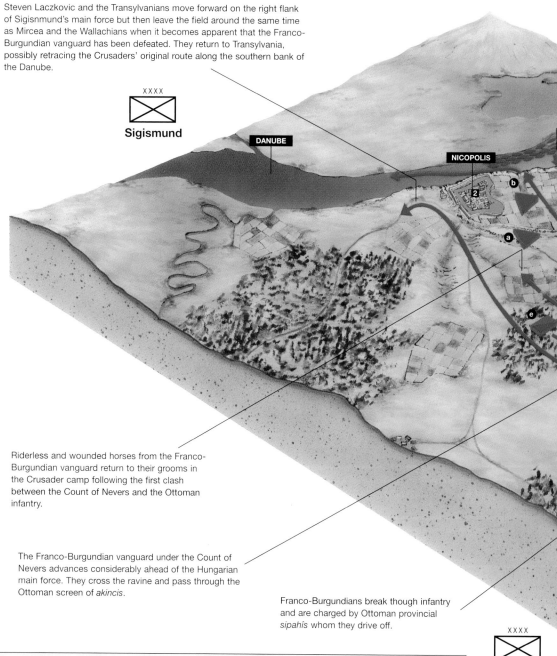

Steven Laczkovic and the Transylvanians move forward on the right flank of Sigisnmund's main force but then leave the field around the same time as Mircea and the Wallachians when it becomes apparent that the Franco-Burgundian vanguard has been defeated. They return to Transylvania, possibly retracing the Crusaders' original route along the southern bank of the Danube.

Sigismund

DANUBE

NICOPOLIS

Riderless and wounded horses from the Franco-Burgundian vanguard return to their grooms in the Crusader camp following the first clash between the Count of Nevers and the Ottoman infantry.

The Franco-Burgundian vanguard under the Count of Nevers advances considerably ahead of the Hungarian main force. They cross the ravine and pass through the Ottoman screen of *akincis*.

Franco-Burgundians break though infantry and are charged by Ottoman provincial *sipahîs* whom they drive off.

De Nevers

OTTOMAN UNITS
1 Ottoman camp
2 Ottoman garrison.
3 *Akinci* light cavalry under Gāzî Evrenos Beg.
4 Ottoman infantry, probably in two corps (Rumelians on right, Anatolians on left), defended by a field of stakes, commanders unknown.
5 Rumelian provincial *sipahî* cavalry, under Süleyman Çelebî and Alî Pasa Sandarli
6 Anatolian provincial *sipahî* cavalry, under Mustafa Çelebî and Qara Tîmurtāsh Pasa.
7 Bāyazîd with household cavalry.
8 Serbians under Stefan Lazarevic.

CRUSADER UNITS
a Franco-Burgundian camp.
b Hungarian camp.
c First position of the Franco-Burgundians under Count of Nevers.
d Hungarians plus minor Crusader contingents under King Sigismund.
e Transylvanians under Steven Laczkovic
f Wallachians under Mircea.

54

396

Ships of Crusader fleet probably move to southern bank of Danube before battle begins.

Mircea and Wallachians move forward but then leave field and cross the Danube to Wallachia.

The Hungarian main force, plus German and other small contingents forming the centre of the Crusader army, move forward to support the Franco-Burgundians, but at some condsiderable distance to their rear.

The Franco-Burgundians attack the Ottoman field fortifications and main infantry position. The Vanguard breaks through the wall of sharpened stakes and splits the Ottoman infantry into two parts.

The Ottoman screen of *akinci* light cavalry move to the left and right, reforming to the rear of the infantry position.

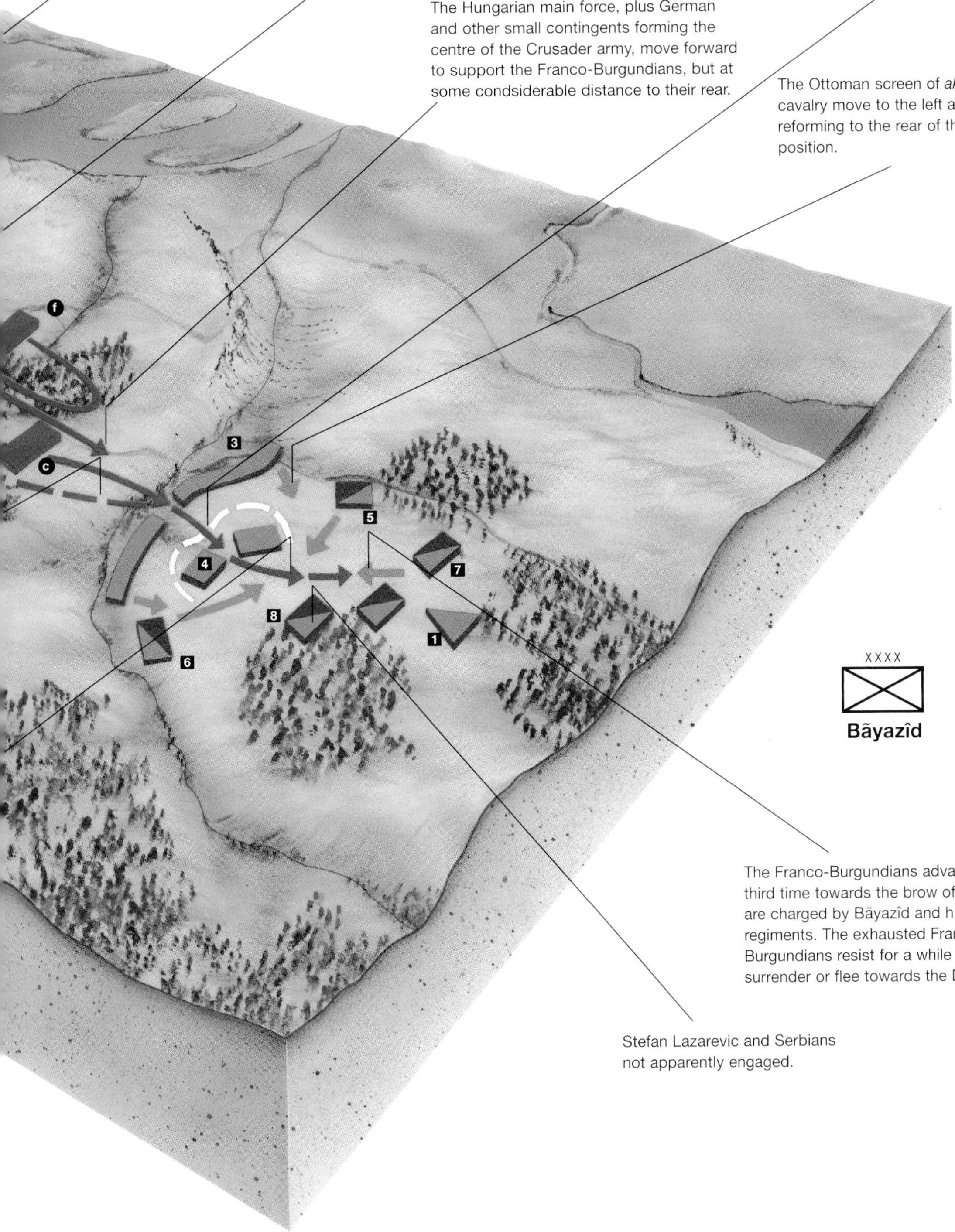

Bāyazîd

XXXX

The Franco-Burgundians advance for the third time towards the brow of the hill but are charged by Bāyazîd and his household regiments. The exhausted Franco-Burgundians resist for a while but then surrender or flee towards the Danube.

Stefan Lazarevic and Serbians not apparently engaged.

Ottoman infantry behind a thicket of sharpened stakes. In reality the *akincis* would probably have shot a few volleys of arrows, drawn the enemy forward and then broken away around the flanks to re-form.

At this point the Franco-Burgundians paused briefly, perhaps taken aback by a steep slope topped by a forest of sharpened stakes and great numbers of infantry drawn up in two large blocs. Today the trees and bushes do not extend up the far side of the ravine and it is easy to imagine that the Crusaders presented the Ottoman infantry archers with a superb target. Crusader chronicles make it abundantly clear that arrows poured down upon the Franco-Burgundians and, according to Boucicault's biography: 'Hail nor rain does not come down in closer shower than did their shafts'. Boucicault also told his men to press ahead and avoid a 'coward's death' from an arrow.

The question of whether the Crusaders now dismounted to climb the slope and uproot the stakes or broke through on horseback is probably misleading and assumes much too much control by the commanders over their men. The slope was steep and in places almost precipitous. Many horses would have been wounded by arrows and thrown their riders. All sources agree that these horses made their own way back to the Crusader camp. As a result many unhorsed Crusaders would have continued up the slope on foot while others were still mounted. Those on foot would have wrenched at the sharpened stakes while Ottoman archers poured volley after volley into their ranks but were probably appalled to find that their arrows had less effect than anticipated. The Ottoman composite bow, though having greater range, accuracy and rate of shooting than the Western European longbow, shot notably lighter arrows and even longbow shafts rarely penetrated the armour that protected the vital organs.

Later 14th-century Turkish epic poetry constantly alludes to the spectacle of European warriors 'all covered in blue iron'. For example the *Destān of Umur Pasha*, written a generation after Nicopolis, but based

The flat plateau south-east of Nicopolis is now agricultural land. (Author's photograph)

The Despot Stefan Lazarevic, in a Serbian wall painting probably made during his lifetime. *(in situ, Monastery Church of Kalenic; photograph Republic Institute for the Protection of Cultural Monuments, Belgrade)*

on 14th-century sources, describes a morning assault by a Crusader army in which 'the enemy dressed in armour and cuirasses, their horse-armour, their mail hauberks were amazing, their gauntlets, their arm-defences, their leg defences, their helmets, all shone and twinkled in the light'. Elsewhere it describes the *azaps* who faced such a formidable foe: 'Some held in their hand a spear, the others a sword, striking relentlessly the blue armour of their foes, while others brandished daggers'.

Within a short time the Crusaders broke through the stakes and got amongst the largely unarmoured infantry. Since the French and Burgundians attacked on a relatively narrow front, the surviving Ottoman foot soldiers were probably forced to the flanks rather than fleeing uphill. Traditional Ottoman histories describe this as a trap into which the Crusaders fell – but if so it was a trap which nearly failed. The Franco-Burgundian corps also dispersed the Ottoman cavalry immediately behind the infantry; perhaps the *akincis* who had re-formed but probably including *sipahîs* guarding the gap between two infantry divisions.

After defeating the Ottoman infantry the aged De Coucy and De Vienne recommended a pause but the younger men, 'boiling with ardour', insisted on pressing ahead, perhaps expecting to find and pillage the Ottoman camp. Instead they were struck in the flanks by the provincial *sipahîs*. A desperate mêlée ensued in which those Crusaders fighting on foot attacked the enemy's horses with their daggers. Heavy casualties were suffered by both sides before the *sipahîs* withdrew to the flanks. All this happened on a steep slope in the blazing sun and by the

As the Crusader army came to the edge of the plateau outside Nicopolis, they dipped down into a deep wooden ravine which separated them from the Ottomans on a hill behind the trees on the right. (Author's photograph)

time it was over the Crusaders, young and old, were tired if not exhausted. The Ottomans were proving tougher foes than anticipated while the French and Burgundians may have realised that the Hungarians were too far back to give immediate support. Nevertheless, they continued up the hill.

At this critical point Bāyazîd's household division appeared over the brow of the hill, shocking the Crusaders, who believed that they had already won the battle. Bāyazîd's cavalry elite crashed into the somewhat disorganised French and Burgundians and, in the words of the Monk of St. Denis: 'The lion in them turned into a timid hare'. Many fled down the hill back to the plateau, others down the ravine towards the Danube where they found broad marshes rather than the river they had seen only five kilometres upstream. The rest stood and fought. Not surprisingly Crusader chroniclers stress the prowess of their own men; French sources proclaiming that Boucicault, De Coucy, the two Sires de

A ferocious attack by the Franco-Burgundian division swept aside the *akinci* light cavalry skirmishers. But when the knights also broke through the Ottoman field fortifications and infantry it looked as if Bāyazîd's plan might fail.

Trémoille, the young Count of Nevers and others were soon surrounded by mounds of slain. The poet Yusuf-i Meddāh provided a dramatic description of battle from the Turkish point of view: 'Among the shouts of Ah! and Hey!, Oh Just Ruler! [God] shouts and the sound of trumpets rose to the sky. Over their heads the clashing of swords. The blows seemed to rain down unsparingly. Fine warriors, in their hands maces, make a rending clashing noise as they fight. Arrows fall like rain and warriors seek room to scatter arrows, the cowards seek to escape, leaving behind their quivers'.

Less colourful Turkish sources merely state that the Ottomans closed in from three sides, which suggests that the provincial *sipahîs* rejoined the fight on the flanks. Perhaps basing his work on the recollections of Ottoman troops who took part in the battle, the Byzantine chronicler Dukas maintains that Bāyazîd's household troops emerged from a

wooded area. Maps made earlier this century certainly indicate that there were many trees on the summit of the hill. The Ottoman chronicler Nesri based his work on statements by the sons of those who took part, stating that one part of the Crusader army fell into a panic, shouting 'The Turks are behind us! The Turks have got behind us!'

Old Admiral de Vienne tried to rally the Crusaders but only ten companions stood by him. Six times, it was said, the Banner of the Virgin was knocked down but raised again until finally the Admiral himself was beaten to the ground, the sacred banner in his lifeless hand. Among others who fell were Guillaume de la Trémoille and his son, Philippe de Bar, John of Cadzaud the Admiral of Flanders, the Sire de Montcavrel (the valiant knight of Artois), Jean de Roye and, it was said, a Grand Prior of the Teutonic Knights. John of Nevers' bodyguard finally persuaded him to surrender. Thereupon the Comte d'Eu, the Comte de La Marche, Guy de la Trémoille, Marshal Boucicault and Enguerrand de Coucy also lay down their weapons, as did several Wallachian noblemen.

Western and Ottoman sources agree that the battle of Nicopolis was actually two battles in which the Ottomans destroyed the Franco-Burgundian and Hungarian Crusaders separately. The precise sequence of events is, however, unclear. Were the French defeated before the Hungarians came into contact, or did the two combats overlap? Sigismund may not have known the fate of his allies once the *akincis* re-formed and the Hungarian King's famous remark to Philibert de Naillac that: 'We lost the battle by the pride and vanity of those French. If they had believed my advice, we had enough men to fight our enemies,' was probably made towards the end of the battle. On the other hand the stream of wounded and riderless horses cantering back from out of the ravine did have an impact on Hungarian morale.

Sigismund, the Hungarians, Germans and other smaller Crusader contingents seem to have moved forward in a vain attempt to support the Franco-Burgundians, perhaps before the latter had surrendered.

The Wallachians and Transylvanians were probably still with them and it may only have been when Ottoman troops emerged from the ravine that Mircea and Steven Laczkovic decided the day was lost. Neither man felt particular affection for Sigismund and both knew that their own territories would soon be raided by victorious Ottomans. Mircea clearly wanted to keep his meagre forces intact, though their withdrawal was naturally seen as desertion by the Hungarians. Mircea's men crossed the Danube, perhaps in small boats which ferried supplies from Wallachia since Crusader vessels moored in the river are unlikely to have helped them. The Transylvanians may have done the same though it is more likely they retraced their steps via Orşova to Transylvania.

Meanwhile Sigismund's corps moved forward, cutting its way through a division of Ottoman infantry who can only have been the *azaps* previously broken by the Franco-Burgundians. The fact that they had re-formed confirms the discipline of the Ottoman army but quite where this clash took place is unknown. There is no evidence that Sigismund reached the field fortifications, which suggests that the Ottoman infantry had moved forwards, perhaps to take the Crusader camp and relieve the Nicopolis garrison. According to squire Schiltberger who was present: 'They were all trampled and destroyed and in this engagement an arrow killed the horse of my lord Lienhart Richartinger, and I Hans Schiltberger, his runner, when I saw this ... rode up to him in the crowd and assisted him to mount my own horse, and then I mounted another which belonged to the Turks, and rode back to the other runners'. This

'Prince Ladislas wrestling with the Cuman (Kipchaq) abductor', *c.*1360. *(Hungarian Illuminated Chronicle, Nat. Szech. Lib., Ms. Clmae 404, f.36a, Budapest)*

THE ROUT: 25 SEPTEMBER 1396

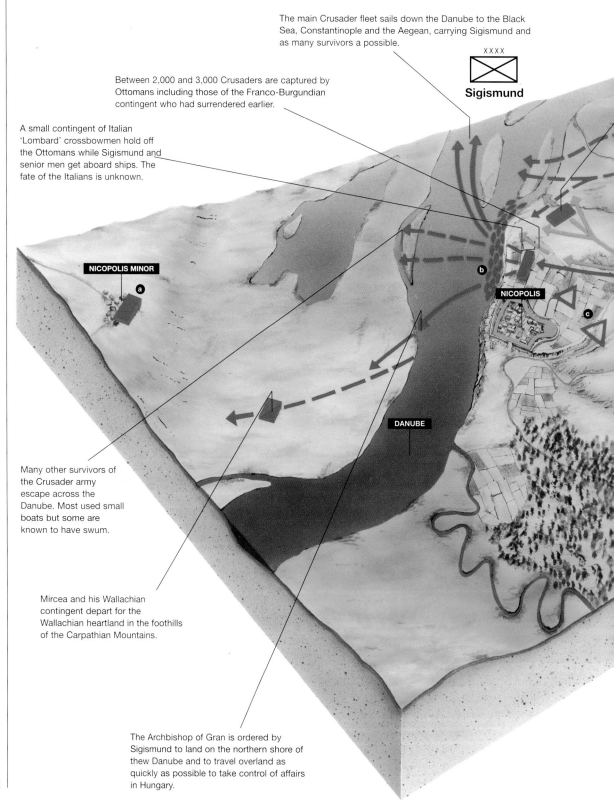

The main Crusader fleet sails down the Danube to the Black Sea, Constantinople and the Aegean, carrying Sigismund and as many survivors a possible.

Between 2,000 and 3,000 Crusaders are captured by Ottomans including those of the Franco-Burgundian contingent who had surrendered earlier.

A small contingent of Italian 'Lombard' crossbowmen hold off the Ottomans while Sigismund and senior men get aboard ships. The fate of the Italians is unknown.

XXXX

Sigismund

NICOPOLIS MINOR

a

b

NICOPOLIS

c

DANUBE

Many other survivors of the Crusader army escape across the Danube. Most used small boats but some are known to have swum.

Mircea and his Wallachian contingent depart for the Wallachian heartland in the foothills of the Carpathian Mountains.

The Archbishop of Gran is ordered by Sigismund to land on the northern shore of thew Danube and to travel overland as quickly as possible to take control of affairs in Hungary.

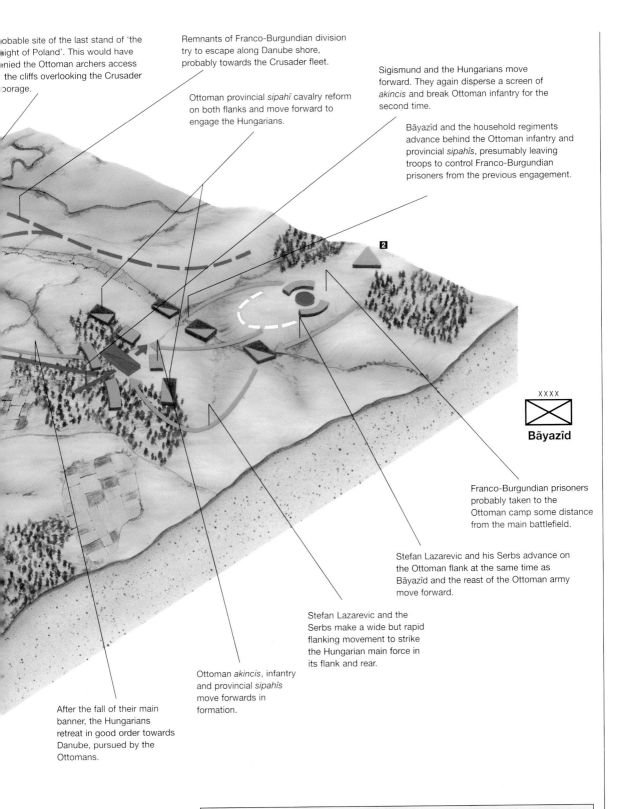

obable site of the last stand of 'the ight of Poland'. This would have enied the Ottoman archers access the cliffs overlooking the Crusader oorage.

Remnants of Franco-Burgundian division try to escape along Danube shore, probably towards the Crusader fleet.

Ottoman provincial *sipahî* cavalry reform on both flanks and move forward to engage the Hungarians.

Sigismund and the Hungarians move forward. They again disperse a screen of *akincis* and break Ottoman infantry for the second time.

Bāyazîd and the household regiments advance behind the Ottoman infantry and provincial *sipahîs*, presumably leaving troops to control Franco-Burgundian prisoners from the previous engagement.

2

XXXX
Bāyazîd

Franco-Burgundian prisoners probably taken to the Ottoman camp some distance from the main battlefield.

Stefan Lazarevic and his Serbs advance on the Ottoman flank at the same time as Bāyazîd and the reast of the Ottoman army move forward.

Stefan Lazarevic and the Serbs make a wide but rapid flanking movement to strike the Hungarian main force in its flank and rear.

Ottoman *akincis*, infantry and provincial *sipahîs* move forwards in formation.

After the fall of their main banner, the Hungarians retreat in good order towards Danube, pursued by the Ottomans.

OTTOMAN UNITS	CRUSADER UNITS
1 Ottoman garrison in Nicopolis.	a Wallachian garrison in Nicopolis Minor.
2 Ottoman camp.	b Crusader fleet probably near southern bank of Danube.
	c Crusader camps and site of massacre of prisoners abandoned.

63

suggests that the Ottoman infantry was caught in the open, probably on the plateau. According to a little known 17th-century Greek chronicle which drew upon lost Turkish sources: 'The archbishop of Vienna [by which the author meant Archbishop Nicholas Kaniszay of Gran] saw the rout of the [French] army, led his soldiers to the centre of the struggle, launched a counter-attack against the Turks and slew many. The Christians were shouting, Victory! Victory is ours! and the Archbishop was able to put the Turkish troops to flight'.

A view across the wooded ravine from the probable position of the Ottoman infantry. The Franco-Burgundian division are likely to have come down the valley in the centre of the picture. (Author's photograph)

After this success the Hungarians took on a body of Ottoman cavalry, probably the provincial *sipahîs*, who would have moved forward with their infantry. Bāyazîd's household division was probably not involved and the outcome was still in the balance when the Ottoman ruler sent Stefan Lazarevic and his Serbs into the fray. They charged towards the main Hungarian banner held by Nicholas de Gara's standard-bearer and overthrew it. Aiming for the enemy leader's banner had, of course, been an essential feature of Islamic warfare for centuries.

Some sources suggest that the Serbian attack was a form of ambush and may have been launched from a wooded area, probably around the head of the ravine since Stefan Lazarevic seems to have been stationed to the left of Bāyazîd's position. If so, it is likely to have hit the Hungarians in the flank or rear. The impact was decisive, as Schiltberger made clear: 'When all the [Turkish] foot soldiers were killed, the king advanced upon another corps which was of horse. When the Turkish king saw the king advancing, he was about to flee, but the Duke of Rascia [Serbia] known as the Despot, seeing this, went to the assistance of the Turkish king with 15,000 chosen men and many other bannerets. And the Despot threw himself with his people upon the King's banner and overturned it'.

BÃYAZÎD'S REVENGE

Once the banner had fallen the Hungarian commanders realised they were on the verge of defeat and persuaded Sigismund to quit the field. At first their withdrawal towards the river seemed to have been in good order, most of the senior men getting aboard ships with little difficulty. A small boat owned by the Hospitallers took the Hungarian King to the Venetian naval commander Monicego's own galley. According to Bertrand de la Brocquière, drawing upon Burgundian recollections: 'Two hundred Lombard and Genoese crossbowmen held off the Turks until the Emperor [Sigismund] had boarded his galleys on the Danube'. Other men made a final stand on small hilltops while others were hunted among the hills. Ottomans who shot arrows at ships as they passed had probably seized the high bluff overlooking the river east of Nicopolis.

Some ships were overloaded and sank but John of Nuremberg, Hermann of Cilly, the Hospitaller Grand Master Philibert de Naillac, the Archbishop of Gran and Sigismund all escaped. John Gara, one of Sigismund's loyal supporters, landed on the north bank and then travelled overland to take control of Hungarian affairs until the King returned.

Many ordinary soldiers were less fortunate. According to De La Brocquière: 'Six thousand Wallachians with the Knight of Poland had placed themselves on a rise a little way off from the Emperor and were

A panel on the golden reliquary of St. Simon made by Francis of Milan for Elisabeth, wife of King Louis of Hungary, in the late 14th century. (Cathedral Treasury, Dubrovnik)

cut to pieces'. Squire Schiltberger saw the catastrophe first hand: 'When the cavalry and foot soldiers saw that the King had fled, many escaped to the Danube and went on board ships. But the vessels were so full that they could not all remain, and when they tried to get on board they [the crew] struck them on the hands so that they were drowned in the river'. Dukas probably based his version on Ottoman recollections, writing that: 'The survivors fled to the Danube where the majority threw themselves into the river and drowned.'

When King Sigismund's division moved forward it broke the re-formed Ottoman infantry and was charged by Ottoman *sipahi* provincial cavalry. At this point Stefan Lazarevic and his Serbs smashed into the Hungarians' rear or flank, overthrowing Sigismund's banner.

Here it is worth noting that, though the Danube is a great river, it was only a kilometre wide at Nicopolis, the water was probably low in September and, a short distance downstream, the river was divided by several large islands. In fact a large number of Crusaders escaped, including survivors of the Franco-Burgundian vanguard. Schiltberger's statement that: 'Of those who could not cross the water and reach the vessels a portion were killed but the larger number were made prisoner' (including Schiltberger himself), might, in fact, be misleading.

Among those who made it home was a Polish knight named Swantoslaus. He probably removed his armour before swimming to one of the Crusader ships, but as he climbed aboard one of the crew injured his hand with an axe. Nevertheless, Swantoslaus still swam across the river and escaped. Other Polish knights who escaped included Stibor of Stiborricze, Thomas Kulski, Demetrius Bebek and John Pasztoh. Sigismund nominated the latter two Grand Palatin and Grand Chancellor in his absence. Presumably they landed on the north bank and made their way back to Hungary overland with John of Gara.

Events after the battle have also been misunderstood or misrepresented, including the number of prisoners who fell into Ottoman hands. They included very senior commanders such as the Count of Nevers himself, Marshal Boucicault, Philippe d'Artois and Enguerrand de Coucy. Western sources offer figures ranging from 400 to 12,000 prisoners. The anonymous Chronicler of St. Denis was an eye-witness and suggests 3,000, while the Ottoman historian Neṣri, quoting a son of Qara Tîmurtâsh Pasa, says that over 2,000 prisoners were taken. He also said that the amount of booty was indescribable. Bãyazîd himself was astonished by the luxury he found in the Crusader camp, where he and

'Iskander and the wolves', a copy of the *Shahnamah* made in Iraq or western Iran around 1390. (Topkapi Lib., Ms. Haz. 2153, f.73v, Istanbul)

his commanders spent the night celebrating victory in one of the finest tents. Unfortunately Bãyazîd also saw the massacred prisoners from Orjahovo and Vidin, and resolved to avenge then by executing his Crusader captives.

The following morning, 26 September, Bãyazîd's anger had not subsided and he ordered all those who had taken prisoners to bring them forward. According to Islamic law prisoners were the property of those who captured them, though one-fifth must go to the ruler. Jacques de Créquy, or Jacques de Heilly as he was better known, was a chamberlain to the Duke of Burgundy, commanded several knights, had fought in the Hundred Years War and had served as a mercenary in the Ottoman army at the time of Murad I. He spoke Turkish and told his captors who he was. So did Jacques de Fay, the lord of Tournai, and both were taken before Bãyazîd. The Ottoman ruler asked them to identify 20 senior captives who would earn the highest ransoms: the Crusaders were so magnificently dressed that the Turks could not tell who was a commander and who a mere knight.

On this basis of Islamic law it is possible that Bãyazîd intended to execute the one-fifth of the prisoners that was his by right. No Ottoman sources describe what happened next, so we only have the accounts of surviving prisoners. They maintain that Bãyazîd ordered all captives to be executed, saving a few who were selected for ransom, but after a period of killing the Ottoman ruler was either sickened or was persuaded that further slaughter would anger God. Estimates of the number of men who were actually beheaded range from a realistic 300 to a fanciful 3000. The Ottomans' revulsion may also have been increased by the way the doomed went to their deaths without resistance, praying to God and encouraging each other to be brave. Those selected for death initially included Schiltberger but he was only 16 years old. According to Ottoman tradition this was too young to die and, in his own words: 'They came the next day, each with as many prisoners as he had made, bound with a cord. I was one of three bound with the same cord and I was taken by him who had captured us'. After the ransomed ones were weeded out, each man was ordered to kill his own prisoners. Schiltberger's companions were beheaded but: 'when it came to my turn, the king's son saw me and ordered that I should be left alive and I was taken to the other boys because none under 20 years of age were killed and I was scarely 16 years old ... Then I saw lord Hannsen Greif, who was a noble of Bavaria, and four others bound with the same cord. When they saw the great revenge which was taking place, he cried with a loud voice and consoled the cavalry and infantry who were standing there to die. Stand firm, he said, when our blood this day is spilled for the Christian Faith we by God's help shall become the children of heaven. When he said this he knelt and was beheaded together with his companions'.

Some of those who escaped overland endured terrible privation. The people of Wallachia and Transylvania were far from friendly, winter descended and the Carpathian Mountains were full of wild animals which also took their toll. Even when the fugitives reached home

Looking north-eastwards down the upper end of the ravine which separated the Crusader army on the left from Ottoman infantry on the hill to the right. (Author's photograph)

weakened men died of disease, including the Count Ruprecht Pipan, who succumbed after arriving at his father's town of Amberg.

It was said that, while the Crusade was away, bad omens were seen in France. A gust of wind blew down the royal tent near Calais and people reported seeing a large star attacked by five small ones which looked like spears – presumably meteorites. In December 1396 the first tattered fugitives reached France. Many headed for Paris where they were imprisoned in the Châtelet as vagabonds and troublemakers. Their tales of disaster were not believed and they would have been executed, but as more fugitives arrived so concern grew. Finally two men were recognised as servants of the Constable of France and were taken before the Duke of Burgundy. They did not have the full story so the Duke sent his chamberlain, Guillaume de l'Aigle, east to discover the truth.

Meanwhile those who escaped down the Danube probably stopped at Genoese Killia to get provisions. The Venetian galley carrying Sigismund and his party reached the Byzantine capital of Constantinople, where he discussed the situation with Emperor Manuel. Sigismund may even have promised to launch another Crusading expedition the following spring, though this never took place. Thereupon the Hungarian party set sail again in two galleys, travelling via various Venetian colonial outposts until they arrived at the Adriatic port of Dubrovnik on 21 December. On the way King Sigismund and his companions also had to endure the humiliation of seeing Bāyazîd's captives paraded along the shore at Gallipoli as their ships sailed through the Dardanelles. Philibert de Naillac, Grand Master of the Hospitallers, reached Rhodes towards the end of December, having less distance to travel, and may have stopped off at various Hospitaller outposts on his way.

At first the Hungarian retreat was in good order but once it became clear that there were not enough boats for everyone to escape, panic set in. Among those who tried to clamber aboard ship was the Polish knight Swantoslaus of Siradiensi. The crew cut at his hands and he eventually had to swim across the Danube.

AFTERMATH AND RECKONING

RANSOM AND UNLEARNED LESSONS

Captivity among the Ottoman Turks was not new for many of the Western European military elite and the prisoners taken for ransom were reasonably well treated. Some idea of the fate of the younger prisoners can also be found in the reminiscences of Schiltberger. But nothing is known about those humbler prisoners who, escaping execution on the day after the battle, simply disappeared. The majority would have become slaves in the Ottoman state or were sold further east. Some would have converted to Islam, earned their freedom and been integrated into Islamic society.

The senior men held for ransom spent most of their captivity in the old Ottoman capital of Bursa. They were fed bread and meat, had some freedom of movement and were even allowed to hunt. Nevertheless, their health still suffered and the Count of Nevers was soon separated from his companions. The Count d'Eu, who may have been wounded, died at Mihaliç near modern Karacabey. He was buried in the Monastery of St. Francis in Galata, across the Golden Horn from Constantinople which suggests that his body was handed over to the Genoese. Here or in a neighbouring monastery other knights who died in captivity or aboard ship from Nicopolis were also buried. The aged Sire de Coucy was also a broken man. Though described as tall and of great strength he sickened and died while the younger De la Trémoille withstood his incarceration best.

It took a long time to arrange ransoms for the surviving noble prisoners. Jacques de Heilly, having been selected by both the Count of Nevers and Bāyazîd, was sent via Milan to Paris with official news of the defeat and a demand for ransoms. He arrived on Christmas Day 1396 and immediately went to see King Charles in the *Hôtel* Saint-Paul. Still wearing riding boots and spurs he knelt before the King and assembled barons to tell the whole appalling story. He also handed over letters from the Count of Nevers to his parents plus letters from other prisoners. In return the King awarded him a pension of 200 ecus but, as Jacques de Heilly was still on parole, he had to return to Bāyazîd. With him went three senior Burgundian knights, the Sire de Vergy Governor of the County of Burgundy, the Sire de Linrenghen Governor of Flanders and the Sire de Château Morand, to negotiate the amount of ransom. Amongst rich presents they took to the Ottoman ruler was a white gerfalcon from the ruler of Milan, since Bāyazîd was known to be keen on hunting, plus fine fabrics and harness decorated with gold and ivory. Jacques de Heilly suggested taking one of those famous tapestries made in Arras, particularly if it illustrated the story of Alexander the Great – another 'world conqueror'.

Before this mission set out, however, French ambassadors preparing to arrange the submission of Genoa to French authority were told to ask the wealthy Genoese merchants to prove their new loyalty by helping ransom French prisoners. The huge ransoms needed for such a large number of the most senior men in Western Europe hit many countries, though France and Burgundy seem to have paid the most through additional taxes. By January 1397 begging letters were already circulating amongst noble families, written by the wives or families of those held captive. Some of the proudest nobility in France asked the Doge of wealthy Venice for help.

Meanwhile Marshal Boucicault and the Sire de la Trémoille were allowed to go on parole to the Genoese Lord of Mitilene (Lésvos) to speed the transfer of money. Both men fell ill and De la Trémoille died. Even when Boucicault's own ransom was paid, he did not abandon the Count of Nevers and continued to urge the payment of what was, in fact, a vast sum of money. Eventually all the ransoms were paid, largely through the good offices of Lombard bankers, the King of Cyprus and Lord Gattilusio of Mitilene, who helped organise the final handover.

As the Count of Nevers and Henri de Bar wrote in a letter to Nicolas Gattilusio, governor of the tiny outpost of Enez at the mouth of the Marica river: 'Very dear and special friend, we have received the 2,000 ducats ... for which we offer thanks with a heart as full as possible ... And we also have the great and beautiful gifts you have sent, including fish, bread, sugar and other things ... We also thank equally your dear and good friend, your wife, for the very beautiful and gracious clothes and wraps which she has sent to us. Written at Mihaliç, the 15th day of April [1397]'. According to the Byzantine chronicler Dukas, Bāyazîd finally allowed his prisoners to go because they left as surety, 'the lord of Mitilene, the son of Francesco Gattilusio'. Whether or not this is true, the Crusader prisoners had good reason to thank the Genoese Gattilusio family.

At last the Count of Nevers could sail homeward, almost a year after the battle of Nicopolis. He stopped first at the island of Mitilene to discuss the future with the Gattilusios and be given new, more suitable clothes in which to continue his journey. Count John finally reached

Dijon on 22 February 1398, nearly two years after he had left. He and his companions also brought some simple gifts from Bāyazîd: a mace of iron, some linen tunics 'in the fashion of the Turks', some bows with leather strings which, for some reason, the French thought was human intestine, and a small Turkish drum. These gifts were not properly understood though the basic message was clear – the Ottomans were warriors who found simple weapons quite adequate, having no need of the splendidly decorated accoutrements Crusaders took to war.

One of the few who had not been shocked by the news from Nicopolis was Philippe de Mézières. Instead he announced that he had a vision in which he saw: 'A big man with a pale face, haggard and disfigured, bare feet, bare head, a pilgrim's staff in his hand on which he leaned, dressed in an old Turkish robe, off white and torn, a cord rope around his waist, a large wound in his left side all covered in blood.' It was the ghost of Jean de Blaisy who knelt beside Philippe, giving him news of a terrible defeat and describing strange visions seen during the battle. He said he was a messenger from the dead and the captives, calling on all Catholic rulers to remedy the situation. This in turn led Philippe to write his *Desconfiture de Hongrie* and *Epistre Lamentable* in 1397.

While De Mézières blamed the sinfulness of the Crusaders, other French writers blamed the Hungarians. Among them was the poet Eustache Deschamps, who, even before the end of 1396, wrote:

> 'Nicopolis, city of pagan lands,
> In these days saw a great siege,
> Abandoned through arrogance and folly;
> Because of the Hungarians who fled the field.'

This was, of course, entirely unfair though the myth persisted. The fame of Nicopolis also stemmed from the fact that the best Crusading army that western Christendom could muster had failed at the first real challenge. It was intended as the vanguard of larger efforts, perhaps led by Kings Charles of France and Richard of England. These never materialised and the Crusade of Nicopolis has been correctly described as 'the last great international enterprise of feudal chivalry'. Instead Crusading became the 'impossible dream' of the 15th century.

On the other hand the disaster at Nicopolis did not dampen enthusiasm among the aristocratic, military and scholarly elite of Burgundy. Instead it inspired greater curiosity about the east, the Turks and Islam. The remarkable voyage of Bertrand de la Brocquière a generation later was largely undertaken in response to the Burgundian defeat at Nicopolis. Nevertheless, Ottoman military success continued to puzzle Western Europeans throughout the 15th century. While the Turks were believed to have inferior arms and little military science, Western forces truly believed themselves superior, particularly in heavy armour and the quality of their horses.

The seal of Despot Stefan Lazarevic of Serbia, c.1410, when he had transferred his allegiance from the Ottomans to the Hungarians. (Manasiya Monastery, Resava)

Seal of an unknown *ban* or governor of Bosnia. (Zemaljski Muzej Bosne i Hercegovine, Sarajevo)

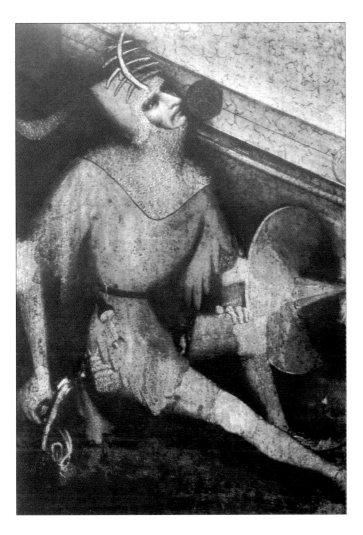

'Guard at the Resurrection' on a painted panel, Bohemian c.1380 (Trebon Altar, Narodni Galerie, no. 0476, 0477, 1266, Prague)

Count John of Nevers' subsequent military career suggests that he learned much from the Nicopolis campaign, becoming the only Valois Duke of Burgundy with real skill in handling an army. Nor did he forget those who had fought by his side. Many were rewarded, others promoted. The crossbowman Étienne Lambin, for example, was made one of the *écuyer de cuisine* and later a Captain of Crossbowmen, leading 81 crossbowmen and six archers in the Duke of Burgundy's service in 1405. He is last mentioned as the King of France's Master of Artillery in 1418. Boucicault was one of the few Crusaders to return east, which he did in 1399 on a small campaign to defend Genoese interests now that Genoa was subject to the French Crown. The recently discovered military plan drawn up by Boucicault before the battle of Agincourt seems to reflect his experience facing Ottoman infantry archers as Nicopolis. It failed against English longbowmen, but did show that the often maligned commanders of French armies could respond to changing circumstances during the Hundred Years War.

Not surprisingly, the Nicopolis campaign had a significant impact on Hungary. It severely damaged King Sigismund's reputation and undermined his already weak authority. In 1401 Sigismund was even imprisoned by rebel barons, though they had to release him because they could agree on no better ruler. More positively, the Hungarian King started a vigorous and prolonged programme of military reform. The *Diet* or 'parliament' at Temesvár 1397 agreed several significant changes, regulating the military obligations of senior churchmen and barons, both of which groups had to provide *banderia* feudal levies to defend the kingdom. More importantly, a *militia portalis* was established in which every landowner had to provide one light cavalryman from every 20 tenant holdings. Whether the majority of these light cavalrymen were drawn from the peasants themselves or were hired soldiers remains unclear, but they were probably equipped as mounted archers. Clearly such a force was designed to face the Ottoman threat. Fortifications along the southern frontier were also modernised with the help of Italian *condottieri* mercenaries. At the same time 15th-century Hungarian chroniclers were less vitriolic about the Ottomans than were those of their Western neighbours. In fact the Ottomans were not described as particularly cruel or wicked. Instead the greatest fear was reserved for their supposed 'false kindness' which 'worked against the soul' and encouraged Christians to convert to Islam.

The impact on the rest of Europe was less. Even so a series of Ottoman raids after Nicopolis reached Styria in southern Austria, sending waves of fear as far as Germany and Venice. On 29 October 1396, when news of the disaster had yet to reach other parts of Western Europe, Venice allocated 5,000 ducats to maintain a fleet to defend Venetian interests in Constantinople. Despite Sigismund's own hostility towards Venice, he realised that the Venetians were essential for future expeditions against the Ottomans. Nicopolis led to greater efforts at co-operation between Hungary, Poland and the Rumanian principalities. Nevertheless, Sigismund's personal rivalry with the King of Poland still led to war in 1410. Worst of all Sigismund found himself entangled in Hussite wars spreading from Bohemia during the latter part of his reign. The Ottoman threat, it seemed, would have to wait.

VICTORY AND THE GREATER THREAT

For the Ottoman army the battle of Nicopolis had been a total if expensive victory. To publicise his triumph Bāyazîd sent batches of prisoners to various other Muslim rulers. Most were from the younger captives, but not all. The German squire Johannes Schiltberger was to have been amongst 16 youngsters sent to the Mamluk Sultan in Cairo. They were led by an older Hungarian knight, but in the event Schiltberger's wounds were too bad for him to travel. Almost 24 years later the Venetian traveller Emmanuel Piloti visited Egypt, where he heard of 200 French and Italian prisoners of war who had converted to Islam, risen to prominence in the Mamluk military system and were currently garrisoning the Citadel. Perhaps they included some of Schiltberger's comrades.

The Mamluk system differed from that seen in other Islamic armies because only Muslims could officially bear arms. Elsewhere non-Muslim soldiers, including Christians, were relatively common. But nowhere were they as integrated as they were in the Ottoman army. Instead of going to Egypt, Schiltberger spent six years as a 'foot page' to Bāyazîd and then six years as a 'mounted page' to his successors. He was captured and recaptured by other Muslim rulers, spending years in the service of various dynasties and travelling through the Middle East, southern Russia, Transoxania

'Soldiers massacre Jacquerie prisoners', in late 14th-century manuscript. *(Chroniques de France,* Brit. Lib., Ms. Roy. 20.C.VII, f.133, London)

and perhaps even northern India. Though technically still a slave, Johannes Schiltberger was treated the same as Christian mercenaries in Islamic service. He retained his faith, no attempt being made to force him to convert to Islam, and met fellow Christians far away in the Caucasus and Central Asia before finally returning to Rome in 1427.

By then the Ottoman victory at Nicopolis had been overshadowed by greater and, for the Ottoman Empire, far more dangerous events. Immediately after the battle Bāyazîd chose not to invade enemy territory, as many of his followers had wanted, but concentrated on consolidating the Ottoman position within areas already conquered. Vidin was, however, retaken, the Bulgarian vassal ruler John Strachimir sent as a captive to Anatolia and his little kingdom incorporated into the Ottoman state. The fortifications of Vidin and Nicopolis were also strengthened, the whole southern bank of the lower Danube becoming an *Uc* frontier march where the bulk of the population was soon Muslim. Bāyazîd also revived the siege of Constantinople.

Ottoman *akinci* raiders, probably led by Gāzî Evrenos Beg, were, however, sent across the Danube into Wallachia. Here Mircea was driven from his throne to be replaced by Vlad, though Mircea marched back with a Transylvanian army early in 1397. Mircea could not regain control of the Dobruja region south of the Danube Delta but Bāyazîd was soon too preoccupied with the threat posed by Tîmur-i Lang to respond to Mircea's return.

Success at Nicopolis did, however, enable the Ottomans to extend their conquests deeper into Greece. In 1397 a raiding force under Tîmurtāsh and Yaqub Pasa ravaged the Peloponnese and razed the citadel of Argos, while in the spring of that year Bāyazîd personally supervised the construction of a new mosque at Veria in northern Greece.

The Crusader defeat at Nicopolis was a huge blow for Emperor Manuel in Constantinople, added to which his mother died in November. As he wrote to his teacher Cydones: 'To prudent men, life is not worth living after that calamity, that deluge of the whole world, but one worse than that [Biblical Flood] in so much as it carried off men better than those of yore!' The Ottoman siege was also pressed harder and Bāyazîd demanded that Manuel hand Constantinople over to his pro-Ottoman rival John VII. Many of the inhabitants agreed and for their part Bāyazîd and his senior officers were so confident that they stood on hills overlooking the Byzantine capital, deciding who would get which palaces after the place fell. In fact the walls of Constantinople and even Galata, on the northern side of the Golden Horde, defied their assaults, after which the siege eased again in spring 1397.

A reconciliation between the Emperors Manuel and John in 1399 calmed the situation, but Manuel's prolonged visit to Western Europe from 1399 to 1403 resulted in no real help. By the time Manuel delivered a funeral ovation for his brother, the Despot Theodore, in 1407 the Crusader army destroyed at Nicopolis had been relegated to a bunch of barbarians whose very names stuck in the throat of a cultured Byzantine gentleman like Manuel, who referred to them as: 'The great army which

TOP **Ottoman helmet of the so-called 'turban' type. It probably dates from the 15th century though this style of helmet had been used by elite Ottoman cavalry since the mid-14th century (National Historical Museum Conservation Dept., inv. 13501, Moscow).**

BOTTOM **Simple Ottoman helmet said to have been found with late 14th- and 15th-century Italian armour at Khalkis in Greece. (Ethnographical Museum, Athens; photo Claude Blair)**

was struck down at Nicopolis – I mean that collected from the Panonians [Hungarians] and Celts and the western Galatians, at all of whose names I shudder at, as an entirely barbaric thing'.

While the remnants of Byzantium withdrew into its cultural shell, other Christian Balkan states dealt with the aftermath of Nicopolis in different ways. The Despotate of northern Serbia survived until 1459 and was even able to expand slightly after Bāyazîd was defeated by Tîmur-i Lang in 1402. Here Stefan Lazarevic threw off Ottoman suzerainty after the death of Bāyazîd, attempted to create an anti-Ottoman alliance and became a vassal of Sigismund's Hungary. In the end, however, Serbia had to acknowledge that the Ottoman Empire was the dominant power. Mircea of Wallachia joined Stefan Lazarevic's anti-Ottoman alliance, supported an uprising in Bulgaria and dabbled in the bitter civil wars that racked the Ottoman state after Bāyazîd's death. But once again, after the Ottoman state was reunited, Wallachia had to accept Ottoman suzerainty. In 1409 the Crusading Order of Hospitallers, based on the Greek island of Rhodes, also made peace with the Ottoman Sultan – for a while.

Whether or not the experience of Nicopolis had any impact on Ottoman tactics is unclear. Since their victory was so complete and the performance of their foes so bad, this seems unlikely. That Bāyazîd's tactics at the battle of Ankara, where he was defeated in 1402, were so similar to those used at Nicopolis, suggested that they were considered adequate. The Ottoman battle array described by 15th-century European observers also continued to be essentially the same as that seen in the late 14th century, though with field artillery and more elaborate field fortifications including a version of a *wagenburg* of wooden carts first used by the Ottomans at Varna in 1444.

Several illustrations in this style have been the subject of art-historical debate. They were probably made for the Ak Koyunlu rulers of eastern Anatolia in the very early 15th century. They also illustrate a form of laminated hardened leather armour used in this region since at least the 12th century. (*Fatih Albums*, Topkapi Lib., Ms. Haz. 2153, f.138v, Istanbul)

Bāyazîd's victory as Nicopolis certainly increased his prestige. Bāyazîd was also helped by having noted scholars at court, including the historian Ibn al-Jazarî, who actually finished his famous verse *History of the Prophet and Caliphs* in the army camp three days after Nicopolis. Ottoman rulers were only officially addressed as Sultans rather than mere *Amîrs* after his victory and this in turn encouraged other scholars, administrators and soldiers to enter Bāyazîd's service. There were plenty of such volunteers now that the eastern Islamic world was in a state of near anarchy resulting in Tîmur-i Lang's devastating campaigns. This influx of administrators enabled Bāyazîd to rule as well as to conquer, but his attempts to change the old Ottoman state from one focused almost entirely upon war against the infidels into an orthodox Islamic empire were only completed by his successors. Nevertheless, Bāyazîd was the first Ottoman ruler to establish a *bîmāristān* hospital, the Dār al-Shifā in Bursa which was opened three years after Nicopolis. The ruins of this complex of wards, bath-houses and rest-rooms for travellers still exists.

Hostile moves by the rulers of Qaramān in Anatolia were punished by Bāyazîd in 1397 and 1398, but this eastward expansion led to a clash with Tîmur-i Lang. In 1402 Bāyazîd was defeated and captured at the battle of Ankara. Nevertheless, his previous victory at Nicopolis gave the Ottomans time to consolidate their position in south-eastern Europe and it was from here that Bāyazîd's successors rebuilt the Ottoman state, re-conquering their lost eastern provinces. It would also be from these Balkan heartlands that later Ottoman rulers launched the amazing series of conquests which, by the 17th century, made the Ottoman Empire stretch from the borders of Morocco to those of Iran and from the East African coast to Hungary and the Ukraine.

The upper end of the ravine between the Ottoman and Crusader armies, perhaps where the Serbs swung left to strike the Hungarians in their flank or rear. (Author's photograph)

THE BATTLEFIELDS TODAY

The route taken by the Crusaders from France, through Germany, Austria, Hungary and what is now northern Serbia and the westernmost part of Rumania can be followed relatively easily, though modern roads do not always follow the line of the Danube. The Crusaders crossing place at Orşova has also been drowned beneath a man-made lake. The route taken by the Ottoman army from their first assembly point near Edirne is more straightforward since existing roads follow similar lines to the medieval roads.

The main area of this campaign, between Vidin and Nikopol, the modern name for Nicopolis, is more difficult. The Danube region of Bulgaria is visited by relatively few foreigners. Nicopolis and Vidin have also suffered from Bulgarian attempts to remove reminders of the Ottoman past. There are rudimentary train and bus services but the most practical means of touring the area between the Serbian frontier

The valley which runs down to the Danube, immediately east of Nicopolis, was probably where the Crusader fleet was anchored during the battle. (Author's photograph)

'The Battle of Roosebeke' in an early 15th century manuscript. This was where Boucicault was knighted. (*Chronicles of Froissart*, Bib. Munic., Ms. 865, Besancon)

Soldiers at the Mount of Olives, Bohemian *c.*1380. (Trebon Altar, Narodni Galerie, no. 0476, 0477, 1266, Prague)

and Nikopol is by car or bicycle, while a hydrofoil service between Vidin and Ruse only shows the river. To quote from my diary of summer 1993: 'The drive from Sofia to Vidin (about 4 to 5 hours) was hilly and occasionally slow but not really mountainous ... Vidin still has its castle but precious little else. They have obliterated the old Turkish town which 19th-century travellers loved so much. They've even built workers' flats in the park around the castle, interspersed with crumbling 19th-century gentlemen's houses and ruined churches. There's still an 18th-century mosque – the only one surviving from a score in the town only 50 years ago but it's shut'. In addition to campsites Vidin has two reasonable hotels, while accommodation can also be found in private houses through the Turisticheska Spalnya organisation.

Again quoting from my diary: 'From Vidin to Nikopol by minor roads along the Danube, the only village mosque I saw was a burnt-out shell near Vidin ... The drive by minor roads close to the river Danube was very picturesque but hard work (again taking around 5 hours). There seems to be only one hotel in Nikopol, in the valley below the citadel hill, cost $4 for a single bed for a night and a cool drink thrown in free (1993 prices)'. The medieval double fortifications of Nicopolis were largely destroyed by the Russians during their three occupations of the town, though the line of an earth-covered wall is visible at the south-eastern edge of the town. Beyond this the visitor determined to find the site of the battle of Nicopolis needs a strong pair of legs, a water bottle and at least half a day.

CHRONOLOGY

1391

Death of King Tvartko of Bosnia; Ottoman troops raid Thessaly and Peloponnese; Ottoman forces defeated by Qaramānids in Anatolia; Manuel II succeeds John V as Byzantine Emperor, becomes Ottoman vassal and fights for Ottomans in Anatolia; Ottomans defeat Qaramānids. Autumn: Mircea of Wallachia abandons Polish alliance and makes alliance with Hungary; receives part of southern Transylvania; Hungarians and Wallachians raid south of Danube while Ottoman forces busy in Anatolia; Mircea retakes Silistria; Serb and Bulgarian rulers drawn into anti-Ottoman alliance; first Ottoman retaliatory raid north of Danube; Mircea accepts Ottoman suzerainty; Hospitallers send reinforcements to Rhodes, Charles VI of France suffers first bout of madness, Philip of Burgundy takes control; Jean Boucicault becomes Marshal of France.

BELOW **Fragment of a late 14th-century Wallachian tile from the castle of Curtea de Arges showing a horseman with an oriental sabre on his hip. (Muzeul National Cotroceni, Bucharest)** BOTTOM **Fragment of a late 14th-century Hungarian tile showing a Cuman (Kipchaq) Turkish horse-archer. (Magyar Nemzeti Muzeum, inv. 17/1848, lost in World War II)**

1393

Spring: Bāyazîd returns from Anatolia and regains control in Balkans.
June 3: Bāyazîd executes Bulgarian Tsar Ivan Sisman and incorporates Tarnovo into Ottoman state; Vidin and Serbia made vassals; Hungarians defeat small Ottoman force north of Danube, take Nicopolis Minor and re-impose suzerainty on Wallachia; Venetian outpost of Tana at mouth of the Don river sacked by Tîmur-i Lang.

1393–4

Winter: Conference of Bāyazîd and Balkan vassal rulers at Serres.

1394

Byzantine Emperor Manuel asks for help from the West; Ottomans besiege Byzantine Constantinople, direct assault fails and is replaced by blockade; nobles of Hungary put aside quarrels with Sigismund to face Ottoman foe.
10 April: Philip of Burgundy sends embassy to Hungary to assess situation.
3 June: Pope Boniface proclaims Crusades against Ottomans and against supporters of rival Pope Clement.
September: Mircea of Wallachia raids Ottoman territory south of Danube.
October: Ottomans retake Nicopolis Minor on north side of Danube, put garrisons in Turnu and Giurgiu, support Vlad against Mircea as ruler of Wallachia; start of four-year truce between England and France.

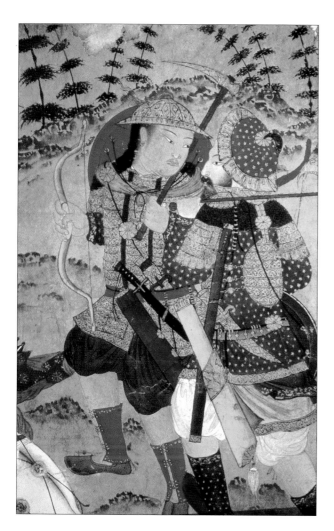

Two armoured infantrymen on a manuscript page probably made in eastern Anatolia at the start of the 15th century. They are probably similar to the *azaps* of the early Ottoman state. (*Fatih Albums*, Topkapi Lib., Ms. Haz. 2153, f.138v, Istanbul)

1395

Early spring; Ottomans raid Peloponnese; Byzantine Emperor sends embassy to France and Burgundy seeking help.

March: Hungarian embassy arrives in Venice seeking transport for Crusade, then to Lyon to meet Philip of Burgundy, Dijon to meet Duchess of Burgundy, Bordeaux to meet John of Lancaster, Paris to seek French help; Venice joins anti-Ottoman alliance.

4 April: Philibert de Naillac Hospitaller Grand Prior in Aquitaine agrees to support Crusade, rival Popes in Rome and Avignon both issue Bulls in support of Crusade.

May: Charles VI of France writes to Richard II of England proposing joint Crusade.

17 May: Bâyazîd and Mircea fight bloody draw at Rovine; Mircea withdraws; Ottomans put Vlad on throne.

June: Queen Maria of Hungary dies; John of Nevers breaks shoulder in a fall from horse.

August: Charles VI agrees that John of Nevers should lead Crusade; Duke of Lancaster abandons projected Anglo-French attack on Turks in favour of official Crusade; Ottomans raid seven towns in Hungary and Transylvania.

Autumn: Mircea ends alliance with Poland, renews alliance with Hungary.

September: rival Byzantine Emperor John VII unsuccessfully attacks Constantinople with Ottoman help, Ottoman blockade eased.

1396

Tîmur-i Lang concludes five year campaign in Middle East and Russia.

February: Alliance between Sigismund and Emperor Manuel's representative signed at Budapest.

March: Grand Master Hérédia of Hospitallers dies, Philibert de Naillac elected new Grand Master.

Early spring: Crusader fleet assembles at Rhodes.

28 March: Burgundian *Ordnances* for Crusading expedition drawn up.

20 April: French and Burgundian Crusade contingents assemble at Dijon, Enguerrand de Coucy and smaller French party head for Venice via Milan.

30 April: John of Nevers leaves Dijon to join Crusaders at Montbéliard.

11 May: Council of Regensburg asked for river transports to take Crusader supplies down Danube.

May: German contingents join Burgundian-French Crusade army at Regensburg.

21 May: Vanguard of French-Burgundian Crusade army reaches Vienna

30 May: Enguerrand de Coucy, Henri de Bar and followers take ship from Venice to Senj, then overland to Budapest.

24 June: Main French-Burgundian Crusade army arrives at Vienna.

July: Various Crusader contingents assemble at Budapest.

Late July: Main Crusader army reaches Budapest.

August: Crusader fleet leaves Rhodes towards Constantinople and mouth of Danube; part of Hungarian force marches via southern Transylvania, Carpathian Mountains and Wallachia probably to Nicopolis Minor; main Crusader army marches along Danube and crosses river at Orsova; Bãyazîd eases blockade of Constantinople and assembles army at Edirne; Ottoman vassal contingents assemble around Plovdiv.

29–30 August: Crusader fleet starts sailing up Danube.

Early September: Crusaders capture Vidin and Rahova, inhabitants massacred or held for ransom; Mircea and Wallachians capture Nicopolis Minor; Bãyazîd leads Ottoman army from Edirne towards Nicopolis and Balkan auxiliaries march from Plovdiv.

10 September: Crusader Black Sea fleet reaches Nicopolis.

12 September: Crusader army reaches Nicopolis, initial Crusader assaults beaten back.

20 September: Ottoman army crosses Shipka Pass.

21–22 September: Bãyazîd collects Serbian vassals at Tarnovo, probably same day Ottoman reconnaissance finds Crusader camp outside Nicopolis.

Probably 22 September: Hungarian reconnaissance finds Ottoman army at Tarnovo.

'The Macedonian army attacks a castle' in a 14th-century Byzantine manuscript. (*Codex of Alexander the Great,* Library of S. Giorgio dei Greci, Venice)

24 September: Ottomans establish camp a few kilometres from Nicopolis, probably on this day a Crusader detachment under De Coucy defeats Ottoman advance guard; Crusaders massacre prisoners from Rahova.

25 September: Ottomans defeat Crusaders at battle of Nicopolis.

26 September: Bāyazîd orders execution of Crusader prisoners in retaliation for the massacre of prisoners from Vidin and Rahova.

December: Fugitives from Nicopolis reach France.

21 December: Two galleys with Sigismund and fugitives arrive at Dubrovnik.

25 December: Jacques de Heilly arrives in Paris with official news of defeat and ransom demand for prisoners.

30 December: French ambassadors sent to arrange submission of Genoa and to ask for help ransoming French prisoners from Ottomans.

1397

Early: Philippe d'Artois dies in captivity.

18 February: Enguerrand de Coucy dies at Bursa.

Spring: Boucicault allowed to go to Constantinople to arrange ransoms.

Autumn: Ransoms delivered to Bāyazîd via Gattilusio of Mitilene.

1398

22 February: John of Nevers and companions return to Dijon.

While most of the Hungarian and other smaller Crusader contingents retreated to ships moored just to the left of this picture, some Poles and Wallachians made a final stand on a nearby hill. It was probably this bluff overlooking the Danube. (Author's photograph)

FURTHER READING

Atiya, A. S., *The Crusade in the Later Middle Ages* (London, 1938).

Atiya, A. S., *The Crusade of Nicopolis* (London, 1934).

Barker, J. W., *Manuel II Palaeologus (1391–1425): A Study in Late Byzantine Statesmanship* (New Brunswick, 1969).

Calmette, J., *The Golden Age of Burgundy* (London, 1949).

Cartellieri, O., *The Court of Burgundy* (London, 1929).

Contamine, P., *Guerre, État et Société á la Fin du Moyen Age: Études sur les armées des rois de France 1337–1494* (Paris, 1972).

Delaville le Roulx, J., *La France en Orient au XIVe siècle: Expeditions du Maréchal Boucicault* (Paris, 1886).

Encyclopaedia of Islam, 1st and 2nd. editions. Entries on: Alî Pasha Djandarli-Zade; Bâyazîd I; Bektâs̲h̲i; Djandarli; Evrenos; Ghulam: Ottoman Empire; harb: Ottomans; Nîkbulî; Sipahîs: in the Ottoman Empire; Tîmurtâs̲h̲.

Gibbons, H. A., *The Foundation of the Ottoman Empire* (Oxford, 1916), outdated but includes Ottoman 'traditional' history.

Housley, N., *The Later Crusades, 1274–1580: From Lyons to Alcazar* (Oxford, 1992).

Inalcik, H., *The Ottoman Empire: The Classical Age 1300–1600* (London, 1973).

İslâm Ansiklopedisi, volume 9, 'Niğbolu savaşi' (Nicopolis battle), (Istanbul, 1964) pp.248–250.

Káldy-Nagy, G., 'The First Centuries of the Ottoman Military Organisation' *Acta Orientalia Academiae Scientiarum Hungarica XXXI/2* (1977) pp.147–183.

Kazhdan, A. P. (Editor), *The Oxford Dictionary of Byzantium* (Oxford, 1991). Entries on: Evrenos; Manuel II (Palaeologus); Mircea the Elder; Nikopolis; Nikopolis, Crusade of; Stefan Lazarevic; Vidin; Wallachia.

Luttrell, A., 'The Crusade in the Fourteenth Century,' in J. R. Hale et. al. (Editors), *Europe in the Late Middle Ages* (London, 1965) pp.122–154.

Nöldeke, T., 'Auszüge aus Nesrîs Geschichte des osmànischen Hauses', *Zeitschrift für Deutschen Morgenlndischen Gesellschaft XV* (1861) pp.333–380.

Oman, C., *A History of the Art of War in the Middle Ages*, volume I (London, 1924) pp.349–52 on the Nicopolis campaign.

Papacostea, S., 'Byzance et la Croisade au Bas-Danube à la Fin du XIVe siècle' *Revue Roumaine d'Histoire XXX* (1991) pp3–21.

Paviot, J. and Chauney-Bouillot M., (Editors), 'Nicopolis, 1396–1996' *Actes du Colloque Internationale (Dijon 18 Octobre 1996) Annales de Bourgogne, LXVIII/3* (1996).

Rosetti, R., 'Notes on the Battle of Nicopolis' *Slavonic Review XV* (1936–37) pp.629–638.

Runciman, S., *A History of the Crusades, Volume III* (London, 1971).

Savu, A.G. (Editor.), *Pages sur l'histoire de l'armée Roumaine* (Bucharest,

1976) includes several articles on the 14–15 centuries.

Schiltberger, J., trans. J. Buchan Telfer, *The Bondage and Travels of Johann Schiltberger* (London, 1879).

Shaw, S., *History of the Ottoman Empire and Modern Turkey*, volume I (Cambridge, 1976).pp.1280–1808

Stoicescu, N., 'Organisational Structure of the Armies of the Romanian Principalities in the 14th–18th centuries' in A.G. Savu (Editor), *The Army and Romanian Society* (Bucharest, 1980) pp.165–191.

Strayer, J. R. (Editor), *Dictionary of the Middle Ages* (New York, 1982–89). Entries on: Jean Boucicault; Sigismund, Emperor; Stefan Lazarevic.

Sugar, P. F. (Editor), *A History of Hungary* (London, 1990).

Sugar, P. F., *South Eastern Europe under Ottoman Rule 1354–1804* (Seattle and London, 1977).

Tuchmann, B., *A Distant Mirror, The Calamitous 14th Century* (London, 1979) on the life of Enguerrand de Coucy.

Vaughan, R., *John the Fearless: The Growth of Burgundian Power* (London, 1966).

'Battle between Bulgarians and Svyatoslav of Rus', Bulgarian mid-14th century manuscript. (Maneses Chronicle, Bib. Apost. Vaticana, Cod. Slav 2., Rome)

WARGAMING NICOPOLIS

In writing these notes, it has been assumed that the war gamer wishing to re-create the battle of Nicopolis will be using traditional war game figures on a playing surface. Such aspects as committee games and role playing have not been considered.

THE CRUSADER ARMY

The Crusader army at Nicopolis was composed of two main elements, the Franco-Burgundians and the Hungarians. There were also some Bohemian, German, Hospitallers and Polish men-at-arms and soldiers in the Hungarian army, as well as separate bodies of Transylvanian and Wallachian light cavalry.

As we have seen, the Burgundian contingent was decidedly the most powerful, perhaps not in number, but in terms of superiority and self-belief. The bulk of the Burgundians were heavily armed and armoured knights, quite capable of fighting either on foot or on horseback. These men-at-arms were supported by a far lesser number of mounted archers and crossbowmen (helpfully, the figure of 13.6 per cent appears in the text), plus some light cavalry. The main thrust of the Burgundians, however, was without doubt the armoured and mounted

'The arrival of the Huns and Magyars in Pannonia' in a manucript of c.1360. (*Hungarian Illuminated Chronicle,* Nat. Szech. Lib., Ms. Clmae 404, f.4a, Budapest)

man-at-arms, confident in himself and his ability, safe in the sure knowledge of his superior social and military status.

The Hungarians also based their military might around their men-at-arms and these were supported by numbers of light cavalry – including horse archers – and infantry with crossbows.

The Bohemian, German, Hospitallers and Polish contingents could be seen to follow the Burgundian pattern, with heavy cavalry and limited numbers of infantry firepower.

The breakdown of numbers between the various troop types is not given, but perhaps if the war gamer uses the stated Burgundian percentages as a guide for the Bohemian, German, Hospitallers and Polish contingents then the resultant army composition may not be too far from the correct picture.

The Transylvanian and Wallachian contingents also included elite knights, some horse archers, mounted infantry – presumably archers and crossbows – plus lighter cavalry.

Assuming the Crusaders' army totalled 16,000 men, we know that the Franco-Burgundian contingent was smaller than that of the Hungarians and others, so it seems not unreasonable to allocate 6,000 men to the Burgundians and 10,000 to the Hungarian contingent.

THE OTTOMAN TURKISH ARMY

The best troops in the Turkish army were the palace corps of six regiments of superbly equipped and heavily armoured cavalry, called *sipahîs*. (Note that for war gaming purposes, these particular cavalrymen will be referred to as '*sipahîs* of the household' in this section of the text, to distinguish them from the 'ordinary' *sipahîs*.)

Throughout the Turkish army, cavalry dominated in prestige, if not in numbers. The bulk of the cavalry were the *timarli*, maintained by fief lords under the *amir* or ruler. Confusingly also called *sipahîs*, these men served with the army from March to October each year before returning home to their farms, etc.

Additional cavalry, unarmoured and therefore much lighter than the *sipahîs*, was supplied by the Turkish tribal forces. Mainly horse archers, these also supplied the frontier or *akincis* light cavalry.

The bulk of the Turkish infantry was found by the *azaps*, but the most famous were the regiments of Janissaries. These were good troops and undoubtedly the Turkish infantry elite.

FIGURE SCALE

Given actual historical armies of 16,000 men, the wargamer has to decide what man/figure ratio to adopt for the re-fight. Much will depend on the figure resource and playing area available, but the following tabulated man/figure ratios will perhaps provide a ready picture:

Army size 16,000

At 1:200	1:150	1:100	1:50	1:25	1:10
80 figs	107 figs	160 figs	320 figs	640 figs	1,600 figs

The forested Carpathian Mountains between Brasov and Ploesti through which many survivors of the Nicopolis Crusade made their way home in winter. (Author's photograph)

Once the man/figure ratio which best suits figure availability, playing area and appearance has been selected, the two armies can be further sub-divided pro rata into the various divisions or troop types.

Taking the 1:50 ratio as an example:

The Crusader War Game Army
The Franco-Burgundians (6,000 – 120 figures)
    103 mounted knights
    17 archers and crossbowmen
Hungarians (10,000 – 200 figures)
    70 Mounted men at arms
    10 Light cavalry
Bohemian, German, Hospitallers and Polish
    70 men-at-arms and soldiers
    10 mounted archers and crossbowmen
    10 Transylvanian heavy cavalry
    10 Transylvanian light cavalry
    10 Wallachian heavy cavalry
    10 Wallachian light cavalry
    Total 320 figures

Please note that many of these numbers are 'manufactured', but are based on percentages and the overall 'look of the thing', which is so important in war gaming.

The Ottoman Turkish Wargame Army
Given the basis that there were probably 10,000 Turkish troops and perhaps 5,000 or so from the Balkans, it is possible to arrive at the following conjectural strengths for the war game:

    50 infantry archers (divided into two bodies)
    60 infantry (including Janissaries)
    10 *sipahîs* (between infantry bodies)
    10 provincial *sipahîs*
    20 Balkan cavalry (right wing)

20 Anatolian cavalry (left wing)
50 light cavalry *akincis*
10 commander's personal guard
50 *sipahîs* of the household (divided into two bodies)
40 Serbian cavalry
Total 320 figures

These figures are at best conjectural, at worst, wrong. It must be stressed that the quoted troop types and strengths, along with the outlined man/figure ratios are no more than suggestions, leaving the wargamer free to adopt, amend or reject them as required.

TERRAIN

The author has opted for the battle taking place on a spur of land fronted by a deep valley, midway between the walled town and port of Nicopolis and a village which one must assume did not exist in 1396.

The Turkish commander deployed his troops on ground that was slightly higher than the main spur, his left flank close to a wood, his right protected by broken ground beyond which steep slopes led down to the marshes along the banks of the River Danube.

In front of the Turkish position was a narrow wooded ravine and the Crusaders' right flank was not far from the head of two ravines which ran beneath the western wall of Nicopolis.

This is a terrain made for supporting a defensive position and needs to be carefully put together to reflect the Turkish commander's intelligent choice of ground. The ground needs in succession to be hilly, sloping upwards, flat and sloping away to the side, as well as providing a ravine. Given the ready commercial availability of such items of wargame scenery as terrain squares of various sizes, constructing a terrain for the battle should not be too much of a problem, although a long, gentle slope is perhaps the most difficult terrain item to construct.

Probably the best option is not to represent this slope, but restrict the movements of the Franco-Burgundians, more of which later.

Wargamers without such luxuries being available will probably need to compromise. The best plan is to assume that the main playing area is the 'flat' ie gently sloping – and add a fairly steep

Unarmoured foot soldiers in an early 15th-century manuscript from eastern Anatolia. *(Fatih Albums, Topkapi Lib., Ms. Haz. 2153, f.138v, Istanbul)*

hill for the Turkish cavalry to initially sit behind. This can be achieved by placing usefully sized objects (in surface area as well as thickness) under the cloth, or building the hill up in contours. No heights are given to guide the wargamer as to how big this hill should be, but we are told that at least the side facing the Crusaders was steep. Three contours placed fairly closely together should suffice.

The broken ground and the slope away to the river are best represented by scattered lichen, with the Danube forming the table edge along one long side of the playing area.

The wooded ravine to the Turkish front and the two to the Crusaders' right could again be represented by the ever useful lichen, with perhaps the extent of the ravines indicated by cotton or something similar.

The rows of sharpened stakes are again available as commercial items, but could be made from matchsticks or a similar material. Laborious but ultimately rewarding work.

DEPLOYMENT

The Crusaders

The Crusaders' plan was to send in the Transylvanian and Wallachian light cavalry to clear the field of *akincis*. The French and Burgundian men-at-arms would then attack the main Turkish force, supported by the Hungarians and other Crusaders.

The Franco-Burgundian leaders were furious at the idea of entering battle behind those they regarded as peasants and were given their way, taking up position at the front of the army. Behind them, along a

The northern end of the Bosphorus straits leading into the Black Sea, seen from Anadolu Kavagi. (Author's photograph)

broader front, were the Hungarians, Germans, Hospitallers, and probably Bohemians and Poles. On the right were the Transylvanians and on the left were the Wallachians.

This meant that the Crusaders' left flank rested near the slope leading down to the River Danube, while their right flank was not far from the head of two ravines which ran beneath the western wall of Nicopolis.

The Turks

The author has stated that the Turkish deployment was standard for the times. Archers were placed ahead of the heavy cavalry, which in turn was divided into a larger centre with two smaller wings.

The Balkan or Rumelian cavalry were placed on the right wing as the battle was on European soil, with the Anatolian cavalry on the left. The infantry were in the centre, protected by rows of sharpened wooden stakes. The Janissaries were probably with the ordinary *azap* foot soldiers rather than being held back with the commander's household cavalry. In front of the stakes were light cavalry *akincis*, who were intended to draw the enemy forward against the main field defences and expose them to cavalry flank attacks.

This late 14th-century Psalter may have been made in Bulgaria or Serbia. It shows cavalry who are clearly under strong Turkish influence. (Bayerische Staatsbibliothek, Cod. Slav 4, f.78r, Munich)

The Turkish commander himself was some distance to the rear behind the brow of the hill, surrounded by his personal guard and with the household *sipahîs* to right and left. To one side of the household division, probably the left, was the Serbian vassal contingent.

THE BATTLE

The Franco-Burgundians, totally ignoring the Crusaders' pre-arranged and agreed 'game plan' at once marched against the Turkish position without informing the army commander. The rows of sharpened stakes halted their advance and the Turkish archers poured their fire onto the Burgundians.

The Burgundians, some on foot by now and some still mounted, forced their way through these stakes and cut up the Turkish infantry who were deployed there, plus some of their supporting cavalry.

As the Burgundians carried on they were attacked in the flanks by *sipahîs* and a bloody mêlée ensued before the Turkish armoured cavalry were eventually beaten off. The tired Burgundians continued up the hill to their front, only to have the Turkish household troops confront them.

This elite cavalry crashed into the disorganised Burgundians, many of whom fled. Those that stood their ground were attacked on three sides by powerful Turkish cavalry. Most were killed but some put down their arms and were taken prisoner.

The Hungarians – including the rest of the Crusaders' army – tried to cut their way through to the beleaguered Burgundians, but were held by the Turkish infantry and cavalry, and totally defeated with the arrival of the Serbians.

A telling victory to the Turkish forces.

THE MECHANICS OF THE NICOPOLIS WARGAME

Nicopolis was a fairly typical 14th-century battle for both the Turks and the Crusaders. The Turkish thinking of the period was to lure one's enemy into attacking and then defeat them from a secure defensive position. On the other hand, the Crusaders' overiding intention, no matter what the agreed plan, was to get to grips with the enemy as soon as possible.

There are a number of points to consider when re-creating Nicopolis on the war game table.

Figure Size

Given two armies of 16,000 men each, with a predominance of cavalry, it would seem that 15mm figures are ideal for re-fighting the battle. The 15mm figure permits the wargamer to field reasonable forces and yet permits a manageable playing area. The terrain and armies for Nicopolis would fit well enough on an eight feet by five feet war games table using 15mm figures.

Moving up a size, the use of 25mm figures provides a more spectacular scene, but requires a much larger playing area, although 20mm figures could well be used without too much trouble. Individually based 25mm figures are absolutely ideal for portraying the Burgundians and their wonderful heraldry, as well as the swooping Turkish light cavalry and the armoured *sipahîs*.

The use of 6mm figures would mean that the battle could be fought on a smaller terrain and the cavalry really could flow around the flanks, but the war gamer would have some difficulty in portraying the ebb and flow of the mêlée.

Commanders

Some wargamers like to reflect their assessment of the various commanders in table top actions and these brief notes have been compiled with this aspect in mind.

Sigismund commanded the army as well as the Hungarian and allied contingents. He was the ruler of Hungary at the time of the battle and possessed great ambition and energy and one could not truly criticise his performance on the day.

John, son of Duke Philip of Burgundy, was brave, wily and ambitious, as well as being the only 14th-15th-century Burgundian ruler who could handle an army successfully. Certainly at Nicopolis he led the Burgundians well as they cut a swathe into the Turkish infantry. It could be argued that if they had not been attacked by cavalry and had conformed to the agreed plan, then the Burgundians could well have won the day.

Bāyazîd I commanded the Turkish army and was a noted soldier. He had a reputation as a brave but impetuous soldier and was nicknamed 'The Thunderbolt'.

Rules

Any set of 14th-century rules should suffice for this war game, but they do need to cater for the numerous different troop types in the Turkish and Crusader forces, so a straightforward 'knight v knight' set might not suffice without amendment for Nicopolis.

We read for example that most of the Turkish arrows, fired from short bows as they were, simply bounced off the armour of the Crusaders. This needs to be considered, as does Medieval arrogance.

Another point is the fact that the Crusaders, principally the Burgundians, had to toil up the slope to reach the Turks, so tiredness should be a factor for them.

One approach might be to use a set of Medieval rules for the Crusaders and perhaps a set of Renaissance period rules for the Turks, as the latter is probably more likely to encompass the disparate troop types.

POINTS TO CONSIDER

Following the Historical Pattern

When re-fighting a particular battle, the forces, the terrain and the deployment at least should all be as close to the original set up as is possible within the wargamer's resources.

Additionally, at least the initial moves of the respective commanders need to be re-created. Unless this happens, then an interesting battle may well take place, but it will not be re-creation of the required action.

How Many Players?

Nicopolis can lend itself to a number of players as a wargame.

There is the straightforward Turkish commander against the Crusader player who must perforce be both the Burgundian commander and the Hungarian commander, but there can be any number of sub-commanders on both sides.

Nicopolis is perhaps an ideal club game – indeed it might have to be, with all the numbers of cavalry required for a reasonable portrayal.

Variables

There are a number of options available to the war gamer to explore 'what if?' scenarios, but in summary the two main alternatives are that either the Burgundians do not charge off ahead but advance with the rest of the Crusade army, or they do go off ahead but the Hungarians fight their way through to them.

These variables are interesting, intriguing even, but bear in mind that any diversion from the historical may be fascinating, but it will not produce a re-fight of Nicopolis.

Knights crossing a bridge of boats in a late 14th-century manuscript.
(*Chroniques de France*, Brit. Lib., Ms. Roy, C.VII, f.136v, London)

COMPANION SERIES FROM OSPREY

MEN-AT-ARMS

An unrivalled source of information on the organisation, uniforms and equipment of the world's fighting men, past and present. The series covers hundreds of subjects spanning 5,000 years of history. Each 48-page book includes concise texts packed with specific information, some 40 photos, maps and diagrams, and eight colour plates of uniformed figures.

ELITE

Detailed information on the uniforms and insignia of the world's most famous military forces. Each 64-page book contains some 50 photographs and diagrams, and 12 pages of full-colour artwork.

NEW VANGUARD

Comprehensive histories of the design, development and operational use of the world's armoured vehicles and artillery. Each 48-page book contains eight pages of full-colour artwork including a detailed cutaway.

WARRIOR

Definitive analysis of the armour, weapons, tactics and motivation of the fighting men of history. Each 64-page book contains cutaways and exploded artwork of the warrior's weapons and armour.

ORDER OF BATTLE

The most detailed information ever published on the units which fought history's great battles. Each 96-page book contains comprehensive organisation diagrams supported by ultra-detailed colour maps. Each title also includes a large fold-out base map.

AIRCRAFT OF THE ACES

Focuses exclusively on the elite pilots of major air campaigns, and includes unique interviews with surviving aces sourced specifically for each volume. Each 96-page volume contains up to 40 specially commissioned artworks, unit listings, new scale plans and the best archival photography available.

COMBAT AIRCRAFT

Technical information from the world's leading aviation writers on the aircraft types flown. Each 96-page volume contains up to 40 specially commissioned artworks, unit listings, new scale plans and the best archival photography available.